Date Due

THE CENTERS OF CIVILIZATION SERIES

ANTWERP
In the Age of Plantin and Brueghel

ANTWERP

in the Age of
Plantin and Brueghel

by
John J. Murray

UNIVERSITY OF OKLAHOMA PRESS
Norman

By John J. Murray

Student Guidebook to English History (Minneapolis, 1947)
Essays in Modern European History Honoring
W. T. Morgan (Bloomington, 1952)
An Honest Diplomat at the Hague (Bloomington, 1955)
Sjomakternas Expedition till Östersjön i 1715
(Stockholm, 1953)
The Heritage of the Middle West (editor) (Norman, 1958)
Amsterdam in the Age of Rembrandt (Norman, 1967)
George I, the Baltic and the Whig Split (Chicago, 1969)
Antwerp in the Age of Plantin and Brueghel
(Norman, 1970)

International Standard Book Number: 0–8061–0893–2

Library of Congress Catalog Card Number: 75–88150

Copyright 1970 by the University of Oklahoma Press, Publishing Division of the University. Composed and printed at Norman, Oklahoma, U.S.A., by the University of Oklahoma Press. First edition.

TO MIKE
Who also loves Antwerp

Preface

Like *Amsterdam in the Age of Rembrandt*, this work stemmed from years of research on Anglo-Flemish cultural relations and exchange during the Tudor-Stuart period, study that led me to an understanding and appreciation of just how important a center of civilization Antwerp really was. What I had felt intuitively from the beginning became more vivid as the facts and details unfolded themselves.

No other town in Europe could compete with Antwerp culturally or economically during the greater part of the sixteenth century. Antwerp was the focal point of much of Europe's history then. Booming in 1500, by the 1560's the city was in a noticeable decline, especially economically. Already the loss of able citizens through emigration was beginning to show. At its heights, however, it was "Venice outdone." From its presses and artists' studios came works that were priceless culturally.

Many scholars have contributed to this volume. The bibliography is only a guide to further reading, in no way approximating the hundreds of authors consulted in this and other studies of mine dealing with Anglo-Netherlands cultural relations in the sixteenth and seventeenth centuries.

Not a few persons have offered assistance and encouragement. I owe most to Louis B. Wright of the Folger Shakespeare Library, whose help intellectually and spiritually has far exceeded that ordinarily given one scholar by another. L. W. Towner of the Newberry Library has also been of help. Professor Leonard Forster of Selwyn College, Cambridge, has offered valuable suggestions. Professor Charles H. Wilson of Jesus College, Cambridge, has read the entire manuscript and—with his broad understanding of Netherlands history—has clarified some of my own fuzzy thinking.

The following have assisted with fellowships and grants which helped make the research and writing of this book possible: The Folger Shakespeare Library, the Newberry Library, the Social Science Research Council, and the John Simon Guggenheim Memorial Foundation. The Board of Trustees and the administration of Coe College have been most generous with leaves of absence. I did some of the research for this book while I was a faculty fellow in the Newberry Library-Associated Colleges of the Midwest Seminar in the humanities. I should especially like to mention Joseph McCabe, president of Coe College, and Blair Stewart, former director of the Associated Colleges of the Midwest.

The unsung heroes of scholarship are the librarians, and many of these have rendered incalculable assistance, giving much of their time and patience. I should especially like to express my gratitude and appreciation to the people on the staff of the City Archives, that of the Saint Elizabeth Guesthouse in Antwerp, and that of the Antwerp City Library, who steered me to materials I would otherwise have missed. My debts to the Royal Library at The Hague, the British Museum, the Public Record Office, Coe College Library, and the Folger and Newberry libraries are large ones. I am especially grateful to the members of the staff of the Cambridge University Library, who have during my three extended stays provided me with services often out of the ordinary; everyone there, from the cheerful porters at the entrance desk to the competent reference librarians and smiling staff, makes working in Cambridge a scholastic joy.

I also appreciate the fellowship and hospitality offered me by Christ College and Selwyn College, Cambridge. Professors L. R. Lewitter and J. H. Plumb at Christ and Professors Edwin Chadwick and Leonard Forster at Selwyn have listened patiently to some of the problems encountered with this book, and for their time, advice, and friendship I am most grateful.

Most of all I am indebted to my wife, Betty, who not only typed the entire manuscript but bore with my ups and downs during composition. She and my sons, Jack and Mike, suffered financially because of my research trips and were often called upon to assume tasks at home that were rightfully mine.

I accept full responsibility for all errors in the book. In the spelling of place and proper names, I have generally used the spelling I saw first, whether it was Walloon or Flemish, except in cases (such as "Antwerp" for "Anvers" or "Antwerpen") where the English spelling is the best known. My love for Antwerp and its people goes beyond linguistic differences.

I hope this book justifies the help, trust, and encouragement of so many people.

JOHN J. MURRAY

Antwerp, Belgium

Contents

ANTWERP
In the Age of Plantin and Brueghel

CHAPTER I

"No other town"

B Y the middle of the sixteenth century, Antwerp of Belgium was the richest and perhaps the most famous city in Europe. Having access to the sea by way of the Scheldt River and to the hinterlands of Europe by river and canals—especially the great canal to Brussels—the city had not only a European market but a colonial one as well. European merchants came here to traffic in goods and spices from all over the world, and representatives of the crowned heads of Europe came begging for loans. The Exchange and the fairs were a world mart for books, crafts, and paintings. Scholars sojourned throughout the city to exchange ideas and search for patrons. Antwerp musicians went forth with their compositions to delight English kings, Burgundian dukes, and Roman pontiffs; and Antwerp Bibles, religious tracts, and preachers influenced both Protestant and Catholic Europe.

The printer Christophe Plantin came to Antwerp in 1549, explaining his reasons for doing so in a letter to Pope Gregory XIII: "I could only have taken my own interests into consideration, and could have assured myself of the advantages I was offered in other countries or towns. I preferred, however, to come to Belgium and to Antwerp above all other towns. The choice was imposed upon me by the fact that for me no other town in the world could offer me more facilities for carrying on the trade I intended to begin. Antwerp can be easily reached; various nations meet on its market; there too can be found the raw materials indispensible for the practice of one's trade; craftsmen for all trades can easily be found and instructed in a short time; moreover I saw to the satisfaction of my faith, that this town and the whole country, shone above all neighbouring peoples, by their great love for the Catholic religion, under the sceptre of a king, Catholic by name and fact; finally it is in this country that the famous university of Louvain flourishes, where the chairs are taken by professors whose collaboration I hope to obtain to the greater benefit of the public."

How right he was and how prophetic. The famous Belgian historian Henri Pirenne has commented: "Plantin without Antwerp would have been impossible. He could become what he became only in Antwerp—and I mean the Antwerp of the 16th century."

Ludovico Guicciardini, an Italian historian who wrote a classical description of the Low Countries, considered Antwerp to be the queen city of Europe. He was astonished by the wealth and riches of the town and the surrounding countryside. In 1557 he found Antwerp "maruelouslie wel furnished both out of their owne countrey and out of forren countreyes, of all kind of victuals and dainties, both for the necessary vse of man, and also for wantonnesse." To corroborate what he had written about the "beauty, grandeur, power, and magnificence of this most noble city of Antwerp," Guicciardini closed his account of the city with two poems. The first was by the scholar Jule Scaliger, Plantin's close friend, who had Antwerp speak for itself:

As many cities as look grimly at me with sinister eyes
So many pale weapons of envy attack us.

London is populous, Paris is industrious, Rome
Is huge, vast is the state of the Venetians, powerful is
Toulouse:
And all the riches and skills both ancient and new
That are in the others are gathered in me alone.

The second was an Italian sonnet by the Florentine Fran-
çoys Pescion:

Antwerp, you enjoy and humbly give thanks unto God
For such a shining and so great a gift
Therefore, you take riches from as many kingdoms
As are in the world, and, happy, rise to the highest.
You follow your course and victoriously spread
To the highest point of all greatness; but it would be good
That the more (note well what I say)
You surpass, and the more power and growth you attain,
That you be the more watchful and jealously guard
Lest your sons, drunk on good fortune,
Destroy such a happy condition.
For if they become haughty, unjust, impure,
Addicted to Bacchus, and with rapacious claws
Short will be your life (alas!) and dire your fate.

From England also came a poetical tribute. On a map of
the city Daniel Rogers (1538–91), who on occasion served
as special envoy of Elizabeth to William of Orange and the
States-General, praised his mother's birthplace as follows:

OF THE MAGNIFICENCE OF THE
CITY OF ANTWERP

Once did ancient Rome bloom with her trophies
And it was renowned for her brilliant temples
But the course of long time has worn everything away

5

. . . .

Rome lies fallen almost with the circuses,
But well does it fall, for a new Rome is rising
Where the Scheldt turns its waters in a whirling current.
See the beautiful buildings of heavy marble rising,
You will say that everything breathes with Roman glory
When you see the good customs and craftsmen.
For unless the predictions of my eager mind fail me
Belgian Rome will not be lesser than the Italian.

Another Englishman, John Johnson, a merchant of the Staple who had avidly read Guicciardini's account of Antwerp, proposed to Parliament in 1571 that the town of Ipswich be made a mart town with all the freedoms of the Flemish city.

In many ways Antwerp was a product of its times. It inherited the commerce of Venice and the Hanseatic League, being on its way up when many other Flemish city were declining. Discovery of the New World and the supremacy of the Hapsburgs helped to determine the course of its history. Ironically, internal wars and religious disturbances, which would be catastrophic factors in Antwerp's decline, helped spread its influence as a center of civilization. To Antwerp during those troubled times came foreigners who tested the city's freedoms and carried away with them new ideas, new crafts, new determinations. From Antwerp refugees and exiles both Catholic and Protestant constantly emigrated to England, the Northern Netherlands, Germany, and other parts of Europe—even to the New World—where they became leaders in the artistic, cultural, and economic development of their adopted lands. At its height, between the years 1477 and

1576, Antwerp was a vibrant, vocal, and violent city with one to two hundred thousand inhabitants, one-seventh of whom were foreigners.

The city was built in the shape of an arc, its flat side forming the eastern bank of the Scheldt River. That arc today, starting at the southern corner, leaves the river approximately where Saint Michael's Kaai joins the Scheldt Straat. It runs along Tol Straat to British Lei and wends northerly along Frankrijke Lei and Italie Lei. Then it veers westerly along Anker Rui, Oude Leeuwenrui, and Brouwersvliet to the Scheldt again.

In 1542 the city underwent a huge expansion program and built its third set of walls. The new defenses were moated and consisted of ten large well-made bulwarks and seven gates, all fortified. These high and extremely thick walls were beautifully made, of white stone with terraced tops of red brick. The elaborate Doric city gates, constructed along with the walls under the supervision of Donato Buono de Pellizuoli of Bergamois, were magnificent examples of work and design in stone and masonry. The new walls were about four Italian miles long. It was about two-thirds of a mile from the crown of the arc, at the river, to the walls, and the walls extended along the river for one and one-fourth Italian miles.

The Scheldt as it flowed past the city was broad and deep and had a tide of approximately twelve feet. Coming off the wharved river were eight large canals where large barques, frigates, and merchantmen could dock, load, and unload. The largest of these inlet canals was north of the city in the newly developed area. This spacious body of water led to the "Palace of the Easterlings" (factory of the Hanseatic League), and it could accommodate more than a

To Borgerhout

To St. Willebrord's & Borgerhout

To Morcxem

To Borgerhout

Kipdorp Gate

Red Gate

St. James's

Horse Market

Kalwenteeg

English House

Princes St.

Bourse

Hessian House

Greyfriars

Catherine's

Kipdorp

House of Aachen

NEW TOWN

Falcon's Cloister

Wool St.

Milk St.

Short New St.

Long New St.

Old Border

To Austruweet

Mud Gate

Easterling House

New Breweries

Great Market Place

Glove Market

Dominicans

Town Hall

St. Walburg's

Vierschare

Sugar Canal

English Quay

Burg

Steen

Baker's Tower

Wharf

Flem

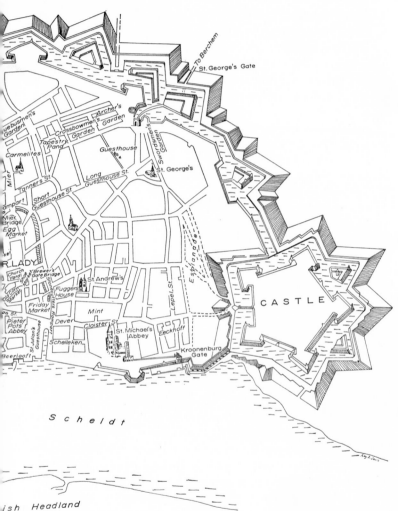

A plan of Antwerp under Philip, with Alva's Castle. Adapted from a map of Antwerp in Jervis Wegg, *Antwerp 1477–1559, from the Battle of Nancy to the Treaty of Cateau Cambrésis* (London, 1916), by permission of Methuen & Co. Ltd.

hundred large merchant ships. Many smaller inlets and canals, spanned by seventy-four bridges, penetrated the city. Today a street name or place name indicates that what is now a paved street was once a quay or a canal.

Within the walls were 212 streets, of which, according to Guicciardini, "the greater part were large and wide and were well known for their straightness and ease for handling traffic as were nearly all Low-Country streets." The principal streets in 1567 were "La Mere (Mier), Langenieu-strat (Lange Nieuw Straat), Kipdorp Straat, Keiserstrat, Coeperstrat (Kuiperstraat), Huyetterstrat (Huidevetter-straat), Camerstrat (Kammenstraat), and Hoochstraat (Hoogstraat)," all important streets in the center of modern Antwerp. By sixteenth-century standards Antwerp and its open markets were spacious, but to today's motorist they are narrow, tortuous, and dangerous.

The main streets of the city were paved, but the constant growth in population caused crowding, especially within the area circumscribed by the city walls of 1314. At times more than ten persons occupied a single dwelling, but the average number was probably eight or nine people to a house. Squalor and filth were widespread, especially in the dock areas and around some of the marketplaces. Just off Hoogstraat, not far from Pieter Pots' Abbey and the Stone-cutters Rampart, was a district known as the "Street of the Stews." One found there a combination of bathhouses, taverns, and brothels patronized by both sexes.

Guicciardini estimated that there were more than 13,500 houses in Antwerp, and that there was space within the new city walls for an additional 1,500, which would have made Antwerp the most populous and best-built city in Europe. Many of the homes had sumptuous and fragrant gardens in the Flemish manner, and all streets and city ramparts, whenever possible, had trees. From the western bank of the Scheldt, Antwerp surrounded by polder country must have been a magnificent mass of pointed gables, spires, and turrets. Dominating all were the bell tower and steeples of the great Church of Our Lady, the city's patron.

Most of the painters of shimmering landscapes and the engravers of city plans and maps failed to depict the struggle between man and nature that was constantly being waged. Only the painter Pieter Brueghel the elder, who glorified man not in his beauty, but in his plainness, and fully comprehended the harshness of life, came close to this. There usually were more people than available living space, and consequently rents in Antwerp were higher than in any city in Europe except Lisbon. Houses with six small, low-pitched, badly lighted rooms plus toilets rented for two hundred écus a year. Better places went for five hundred écus and up. All had the narrow passages and steep stairs characteristic of houses in the Low Countries. The crowding, which recurred in spite of local ordinances regulating rentals and the housing of servants, was detrimental to both health and morals. Servants often included staffs of workmen and their families attached to some concern, such as the printers and typesetters in Plantin's shop and bindery.

Crowding was conducive to plague, that scourge of medieval and Renaissance man. Sieges of sweating sickness, some of the worst in the history of western Europe, hit Antwerp in 1480, 1485, 1517, 1529, and 1551. Although the disease took a heavy toll of rich as well as poor, the poor paid most dearly. When the ministrations of the medical profession proved ineffective, many people turned to faith as their only recourse, and religious processions, some numbering over a thousand persons—many of them high dignitaries—jammed the streets. The "Netherlands" treatment of throwing victims into a violent sweat increased the number of deaths. Erasmus, who was in Antwerp in 1517, complained that pills he had taken had made him ill, and a friend warned him that physicians often made no distinction between a human and a horse. Even worse than the physicians were the untrained quacks who preyed on the hopes of the desperate. To cut down abuses of this kind, strict ordinances forbade practice by nonlicensed physicians.

Diseases other than plague—caused by poor water, bad sanitation, and abysmal ignorance—added to the overwhelming number of deaths in Antwerp. Death by fire was also a constantly lurking danger. In 1441 many parts of Antwerp in the Wolstraat area went up in flames, and two years later a district along Hoogstraat was leveled. In these areas most of the houses had been built of wood with thatched roofs. The new buildings were safer than the old. The rooms were often low pitched with small windows, the upper stories jutting out one over the other. Although built of brick, their ornamental wooden fronts were fire hazards, and the inhabitants were fond of growing vines on their houses. This practice was forbidden by the magistrates, not only because of danger from fire, but also because of quarrels among the burghers over ownership of the fruit.

There were so many fires in 1503 that the magistrates were compelled to take measures for the public safety. They ordered that tubs of water be placed in front of all doors, and that thatched roofs on those streets through which religious processions passed be tiled within six years. Houses built on other streets were required to have tile roofs within ten years. Subsequent edicts outlawed wooden fronts and prohibited the building or repairing of any house with wood. Walls of structures were required to be at least a foot thick above ground. In spite of these precautions, the worst fire took place in 1541. It originated in Maelderij-straat and consumed some thirty houses located in the street of the Great Market and in the churchyard of Our Lady. Among the greatest losses was the Old Cloth Hall with its velvets, silks, and damasks.

Other hardships were extremes of drought and flood. A long dry spell in the surrounding agricultural hinterland would lead to food shortages, even famine, a threat that constantly hovered over sixteenth-century man. Although 1518, a year of good harvests, was a year of plenty in the city, six years later there was a serious shortage of bread. Other lean years because of drought and cold weather were 1545, 1546, 1556, and 1565. Naval blockade, international politics, and constant conflict made lean times even leaner.

Heavy rains and high tides destroyed quay, house, property, and life. In Roman times, Antwerp was probably inundated. Although much of the city and surrounding land depended on dikes to keep back the sea, sometimes rising water driven landward by angry tides was too much for man-made defenses. In 1480, 1530, 1532, and 1552 heavy floods caused acute distress in many areas of the city. In 1552 there were two severe inundations.

War, portrayed by the painter and Antwerpian visitor Albrecht Dürer as the Fourth Horseman of the Apocalypse, at times ravaged the city. Riot increased the chaos of war, and throughout the sixteenth century the city suffered from enemies within and without its walls. Self-styled friends often did more damage to the city than overt foes. In the long series of wars between Hapsburg and Valois from 1477 to 1559, for example, Flanders was a primary battleground, as it was to be later in the struggles between

13

France and Germany. The Treaty of Cateau-Cambrésis, April 7, 1559, brought a brief respite to the Hapsburg-Valois rivalry, but this truce was the prelude to the Eighty Years' War which was to devastate the Low Countries and cause Antwerp to lose its prominant position. The gravest outside threat prior to the Eighty Years' War occurred in 1542 when the Guelders General Martin van Rossem—whose mercenaries ranged from Swedes to Frenchmen—led forces for William of Cleves against the city. Although the countryside was ravaged and the walls were breached, the city held, repulsing the invader after a bitter struggle.

Internal unrest and rioting probably caused more damage than actual warfare. In 1477 the Antwerpians had attempted to throw off the yoke of Mary of Burgundy in the "Quaey Wereld" uprising, only to be squelched in 1483 by Mary's husband, Maximilian of Hapsburg, soon to be Holy Roman emperor. In 1566 zealous and bigoted Protestant vandals, in the name of religion, sacked many of the churches and religious foundations in the city. Ten years later, in November, 1576, the city suffered its worst sacking when unpaid Spanish troops stormed out of the Antwerp fortress and ran mad through the city streets. "The Spanish Fury" paralyzed the economy, burned at least a thousand homes, plundered and destroyed public and private property valued at six million florins, and killed at least eight thousand citizens. Plantin, like some others, was able to save his printing establishment from plunder and destruction only by ransoming the property. Neither he nor Antwerp ever recovered fully from this disaster. The next year a "German Fury" was barely averted, but in 1583, French troops supposedly protecting the citizens from the Spanish loosed the "French Fury" upon the city. From 1584 to 1585 Antwerp was blockaded and besieged by the Spanish

General Alexander Farnese, duke of Parma. On August 17, 1585, the city capitulated. Although later besieged by various members of the House of Orange and North Netherlands troops, Antwerp remained in non-Flemish hands, with its liberties—economic, political, religious—sharply curtailed. Man had succeeded in bringing the proud city to its knees after flood, fire, and disease had failed.

Before this final calamity, however, Antwerp, in the middle of the century, underwent a great building period. Construction of the new walls, promise of political and religious refuge, easy citizenship, and lust for gain and profit brought newcomers to the city in large numbers. New homes, warehouses, shops (*panden*), guild halls, places of residence and trade for foreign merchants, exchanges, churches, and other buildings were in great demand. Needs and shortages led to speculative booms in real estate and building. Among the entrepreneurs so engaged on a large scale were the Gilbert van Schoonbekes (father and son), Hubert de But, Jacques van Hencxthoven, Gérard and Thomas Grammaye, and Herman Boelman.

Gilbert van Schoonbeke the son (1519–56) was a businessman, engineer, and town planner. The illegitimate son of an Antwerp merchant, he was called by contemporaries the "Meliorator" and the "Reconstructor" of Antwerp. No man deserved these titles more. It is impossible to walk through the city with a competent guide without hearing his name.

Gilbert assumed the business interests as well as the name of his father, and in 1544 became legitimized by Charles V at a time when Antwerp was expanding. From 1542 to 1548 he bought for his private ownership various buildings and properties and soon surpassed his father as a business-

man. On these properties he laid out streets and markets—
such as the rue des Lombards, the rue du Canal, the rue des
Juife, the Tuesday Market and adjacent streets, the new
Weigh House, the new Moriaen, the rue de la Lunettee,
and adjoining streets—and built brick-making foundries
and a large number of villas.

At the time, Antwerp was suffering severe growing
pains. Expansion of the city's walls in 1542, which cost one
million crowns, threatened to wreck the city's economy.
In spite of import taxes on wine and beer, taxes on houses
already constructed and those to be built, taxes on land,
sales, purchases, and misdemeanors, and even a personal tax,
the city was unable to meet financial demands by the emperor. Money from outside was difficult to come by, and
Italian bankers were holding out for exorbitant interest
rates. The city itself, the world's money mart, was facing
bankruptcy.

The pensionary of Antwerp, Jacques Maes, called
Charles V's attention to van Schoonbeke, and the emperor
commissioned the builder to solve the problem. With
characteristic daring, Gilbert reorganized the original city
plans by parceling and selling plots, tracing new streets,
constructing new buildings, and finishing the fortifications.
In addition, he provided canals, quays, and other commercial advantages unthought of previously. This ingenious
engineer made Antwerp the best-furnished seaport in
northern Europe.

Gilbert signed a contract February 5, 1549, for the resale
of property belonging to the city. He promised to procure
for the city within four years the sum of three hundred
thousand florins in gold or in rents, or forfeit his remunera-
tion. He reduced the number of canals (*vlieten*) to three,
all inlet extensions of the Scheldt. These were the Brewers'

Canal (Brouwersvliet), the Middle Canal—later Eastern Canal (Oosterse vliet), since it lay near the factory of the Hanseatic merchants (House of the Easterlings)—and the Carpenter's Canal (Timmervliet). The first of these was vaulted in 1882, and was the last of the Antwerp canals to disappear in this way.

Fearing financial loss, van Schoonbeke modified his plan on February 17, 1551. He contracted to build the Croonenburg Bridge and six hundred rods of fortification on the north side of the city where the city walls were to meet the Scheldt. He also agreed to do the masonry work on the canals and to build a part of the Tapissierspand, in which were later sold the renowned rugs and carpets of this period. He promised to pave the rue d'Aremberg at a price ranging from 14 to 26 florins a rod, as compared with an earlier cost of 30 to 36 florins a rod. In payment van Schoonbeke was to receive from Antwerp 300 plots of land in the Schuttershoven (the garden of the military guild) and 150 plots in the New Town. Schoonbeke guaranteed Antwerp 144,000 florins for its building properties and 180,000 florins if the city would add the English House near the Old Bourse (Oude Beurs). He promised that if there should be a deficit in the guaranteed income, he would underwrite a part of the loss. If the income exceeded expectations, he would share a part of the general prosperity.

To make the sites of the New Town financially more attractive, Schoonbeke established breweries there—to stimulate the economic activity of the new district and to increase Antwerp's revenues from the beer excise. Since brewing was good business, there being an acute beer shortage in the city, van Schoonbeke established other breweries in the old part of Antwerp. When the new district was unable to supply sufficient water for Gilbert's far-flung enterprises, he constructed a waterhouse to which water would be brought by special pipe and distributed through smaller pipes to the neighborhood breweries. This remarkable building became the Brewer's Guild Hall and operated until about 1930, when it was converted into a museum. Over the years the motive power changed from horses to electricity, and pipes from wooden to leaden. In 1763 a visitor commented that water was drawn up seventy feet from the basin to the upper reservoir, the waterhouse supplied a thousand tons of water an hour, and "The beer is very delicious and cheap."

Unfortunately for Gilbert, ten of his breweries were completed before the Waterhouse could be put into operation, and he was obliged to import water by barge from Rumst on the river Rupel, an affluent of the Scheldt. The envious brewers in the Old Town spread the rumor that this water had "a bad smell" and that "a kind of maggot came into the beer." Gilbert also treated craft regulations dealing with the recruitment of workmen and the gathering of materials in cavalier fashion. His prices were lower and profits higher than those of many of his contemporaries. On July 12, 1554, a segment of the populace turned against Gilbert and his friend Jacob Maes, and the two were forced to take refuge in the Town Hall, where a soldier who defended them, Herman Weerts, was mortally wounded. Van Schoonbeke and Nicholas Maes, a relative of Jacob's who had been responsible for collecting the excise taxes, were expelled from the city. Although Charles V returned with troops and crushed the rebels, the role of Gilbert in Antwerp was ended. He carried out confidential missions for the emperor and maintained an Antwerp residence, "De Keyser," on the present-day Minderbroedersrui ("Minorite Canal"), where he died in December, 1556, at the age of thirty-seven. His Waterhouse and his enterprises continued according to plan, and his work epitomizes the economic daring and architectural growth of the city.

Other architects and masterbuilders, foreign-born and native, were plentiful in sixteenth-century Antwerp. Among these were Herman de Waghemakere and his son Dominic, Rombaut Keldermans, and John van Vlierden, alias de Nimègue. Engineer carpenters—such as Pierre Frans, Phillip Lammekens, Rombaut de Dryvere, Lambert van Noort—also made substantial contributions to sculpture and building in Antwerp.

Peter Coeck van Aalst introduced the Renaissance style into Antwerp, translating the work of the Italian architect Sebastiano Serlio of Bologne into Flemish. He was aided in his campaign to introduce Italian ideas by François de Vriendt (Floris) and his pupil Martin de Vos, followed by Guillaume Boyen, John Buchner, Guillaume Paludanus, and the Spillemans, who were all master masons and Antwerpians. Among the outsiders employed by the city were Henré von Pide, Louis van Beughem, Jon Mynsheeren, and Donato Buono de Pellizuoli.

As in many Netherlandish towns, lack of land often dictated building style. Lots were usually narrow and deep. The general tendency was to lay down the frames of the structure on the width of the house and to enclose the roof by a gable façade at each end. Antwerp houses even during the Renaissance were generally built in the form of an equilateral triangle. The Renaissance style with covering of a wing by a rafter with a leading edge was used only toward the end of the sixteenth century and usually on public or commercial buildings or on the spacious homes of the rich. This style was distinguished by plain vaults on the entry doors and the doors of the wings, which had embossed imposts and keystones, and by flat moldings on the windows and cordons at different stories. The first major construction in this style was the Mason's Guild Hall erected on the Cheese Canal in 1531. The Vierschare ("Court of Justice") was built according to the new tastes in 1540, as was the house of the Hansa and that of Celle.

Although steeped in the Italian tradition, Guicciardini was tremendously impressed by the architectural achievements of the Antwerpians, whom he considered to be great builders. "Many goodly buildings there are in Antwerp," he wrote, "as well private as publike, but the publike especiallie are very sumptuous, namely, the place where Arras is solde, the Butchery, the Waighouse, the English house, many sumptuous ware houses built for the English men, the newe lodging for the discharging of Marchandise that commeth to the towne by lande, but the Easterlings lodging passeth all these in greatnesse and magnificense, yet is that as farre surmounted by the townehouse, the building wherof, cost almost 100000. crownes."

The homes of the wealthy, the envy of foreigners, were a testimony to the opulence of the owners and the artistic genius of the builders. Some of these, such as the House of Plantin, are extant today and have been converted into city museums. Also extant with lovely frontage and grand tower is the magnificent domicile built by Dominic de Waghemakere on the Prinsstraat for the burgomaster Arnold van Lierre. Warehouses were built onto the residential part of the building, but they did not detract from the grandeur of the structure or the spirit and beauty of its gardens. Dürer wrote in 1520:

"On Saturday after the feast of St. Peter in Chains my host took me to see the burgomaster's [Arnold van Lierre] house at Antwerp. It is newly built and beyond measure large, and very well ordered, with spacious and exceedingly beautiful chambers, and many of them, a tower splendidly ornamented, a very large garden . . . altogether a noble house, the like of which I have nowhere seen in all Germany. The house also is reached from both sides by a very long street, which has been quite newly built according to the burgomaster's liking and at his charges."

Dürer also commented on Jacob Fugger's house: "He has newly built it in very costly fashion with a noteworthy tower, broad and high, with a beautiful garden."

The house Degroote Zot ("Big Fool") built by the town treasurer William de Moelenere in 1554 on Saint James's Market contrasts sharply with the house of van Lierre. Now the Royal Flemish Academy of Music, its overhanging ledges, elaborately carved triangular supports, flamboyantly colored iron-framed windows and highly ornamented friezes, and open and spacious courtyard are forerunners of Renaissance building. Peter Coeck van Aalst did the interior. The richly carved and colored chimney pieces, the walls hung with tapestry and leather, the painted ceilings, and the windows filled with colored glass are representatives of the new tastes popular in Antwerp during the late sixteenth century. Indeed, color is the keynote of the whole period. Renaissance influences are apparent in the statues and figures which beautified the gardens, courtyards, and galleries. Ornate chimney pieces, caryatids, figures of angels, and floral decorations were the vogue.

Public building in Antwerp during the sixteenth century generally fell into three categories—religious, civic, and commercial. Prior to Martin Luther, Antwerp was overrun with religious foundations and orders, all with their own building programs. Ecclesiastical architecture ranged from the magnificent Saint Elizabeth Guesthouse to Antwerp's four parish churches. Saint Walburge's may have been the oldest church in the city, and Saint James's perhaps the most beautiful, but the most magnificent was the great parish Church of Our Lady (Onze Lieve Vrouwekerk). It was the largest parish church in Christendom, and when it was raised to the dignity of a cathedral in the second half of the sixteenth century, it could be rivaled in its new category only by the church at Cologne. After a fire in 1533, the church was rebuilt rather much in its present form according to plans of Dominic de Waghemakere and Rombaut Keldermans. Although Antwerp ecclesiastical foundations suffered badly during the religious conflicts, church construction continued throughout the entire sixteenth century, influenced by the spirit of the Renaissance.

The best extant civic building in the old Flemish Gothic style is the Vleeshuis ("Butcher's Hall"), which was built between the years 1500 and 1503 on the Vleeshouwersstraat near the cattle market. It was designed by Herman de Waghemakere and is now a museum. During its heyday it was a place where the Butcher's Guild sold its meat. The guild decorated its building handsomely, and its stepped gables are a reminder that many guild halls before the Renaissance were built in this manner. It is an interesting pleasing specimen of civic architecture, witih a gable and turrets surmounted by spires, and is built of bricks in rows alternating with lines of stone.

The Great Market Place and the dominating Stadthuis ("Town Hall") represented both Gothic and Renaissance styles. The old Stadthuis, not on the site of the present building, was in pointed style, made of wood with a stone façade. The stepped gable was flanked by four towers, and there were two towers in the back façade. This structure dominated the scene in the first half of the century. It was no larger than those town halls found in smaller towns, and it was not 150 years old when it became so unsafe that "to tremble like the Town Hall" became a familiar saying. It may have been damaged by the fire of 1541, which consumed the neighboring Cloth Hall buildings in the Market Place and others in the churchyard of Our Lady's Church.

The new Stadthuis building was constructed by Cornelis de Vriendt (brother of Floris) between 1561 and 1564 according to plans by Hans Vredeman de Vries. Not only did the Town Hall follow the new flamboyant Renaissance architecture, but many nearby guild halls, such as the Cloth Hall, were also constructed in this style. Man has destroyed most of this area, but the reconstruction was done according to the specifications of the late sixteenth century, so that buildings in this area today are replicas instead of originals. But they do show the tastes of the Renaissance. At the Great Market Place, the very soul of the city, one can find examples of Gothic and early Renaissance as it came to Flanders.

A tourist attraction in the sixteenth century was the New Bourse, erected by Dominic de Waghemakere in 1531 between the Mier and Long New Street. The new construction in general followed plans made by Dominic for an earlier Bourse that had been built in 1515 on Wool Street, now the Old Bourse. The Old Bourse, still standing, had a gallery which jutted out over two of its four sides and was supported by eight cylindrical stone columns. Flamboyant in style, it had one tower.

The New Bourse, which cost Antwerp the staggering sum of three hundred thousand golden crowns, was considered to be one of the most remarkable buildings in the world. Guicciardini thought that as a meeting place for merchants it had no equal in the world. The building was a rectangular court, around the sides of which stretched a portico resting on thirty-eight sculptured columns, no two of which were alike in ornamentation. Two towers crowned the building, and above the Bourse were shops, where at a later period painters sold their works. This structure was destroyed by fire in 1581, and another building was constructed which subsequently met a similar fate. The present Bourse, opened in 1872, resembles the New Bourse built by de Waghemakere.

The Antwerp Bourse became the prototype for all similar edifices raised in Europe. Correspondence between Sir Thomas Gresham and his agent Richard Clough shows to a surprising extent how much the English Bourse and subsequent English buildings were indebted to Antwerp and other Flemish towns for design, decorations, and materials. "Sir Thomas employed a Fleming, Henryk, for the building of the Burse . . . and all the materials down to the statue of Queen Elizabeth and the paving stones were shipped from Antwerp under his direction."

It was a colorful city, this Antwerp, and alive with activity. The many marketplaces abounded with people from all over Europe and even outside the continental limits of Europe, and with goods from the overloaded stalls of the traders. An army of stevedores was required to unload the ships bulging with products from the European ports. Their shouts and curses blended with the church bells. The hoarse songs of the sailors heaving anchor provided a harmonious background for voices of hurrying porters and cries of itinerant vendors.

The diverse languages of the merchants created a babel of tongues, and their costumes were a kaleidoscope of colors and styles. Ships and cargoes, seamen and traders move inward and outward, bound for the corners of the world. The striding of the guards assigned to man the ramparts, the Joyous Entry of the sovereigns into the city, the pomp and ceremony connected with the opening of the fairs—almost all accompanied by architectural designs, fireworks, and processions—must have amazed foreigners. Churchmen and thieves, ladies and fishwives, nuns and prostitutes encountered each other at almost every corner.

Crime was widespread, and the punishment of criminals was always exciting to the somewhat brutal population. The great spectacles, however, were religious, the most important being the procession of the Feast of the Circumcision, during which a most remarkable relic was carried through the city.

Both Guicciardini and Dürer have left us full accounts of religious processions. The latter's account of the celebration of the Assumption of the Virgin is as follows:

"On the Sunday after our dear Lady's Assumption I saw the great procession from the Church of Our Lady at Antwerp, when the whole town of every craft and rank was assembled, each dressed in his best according to his rank. And all ranks and guilds had their signs, by which they might be known. In the intervals great costly pole-candles were borne, and their long old Frankish trumpets of silver. There were also in the German fashion many pipers and drummers. All the instruments were loudly and noisily blown and beaten.

"I saw the procession pass along the street, the people being arranged in rows, each man some distance from his neighbour, but the rows close one behind another. There were goldsmiths, the painters, the masons, the broiderers, the sculptors, the joiners, the carpenters, the sailors, the fishermen, the butchers, the leatherers, the clothmakers, the bakers, the tailors, the shoemakers—indeed workmen of all kinds, and many craftsmen and dealers who work for their livelihood. Likewise the shopkeepers and merchants and their assistants of all kinds were there. After these came the shooters with guns, bows, and crossbows, and the horsemen and foot soldiers also. Then followed a great crowd of the lords magistrates. Then came a fine troop all in red, nobly and splendidly clad. Before them, however, went all the religious orders and the members of some foundations very devoutly, all in their different robes. A very large company of widows also took part in this procession. They support themselves with their own hands and observe a special rule. They were all dressed from head to foot in white linen garments, made expressly for the occasion, very sorrowful to see. Among them I saw some very stately persons. Last of all came the chapter of Our Lady's Church, with all their clergy, scholars, and treasures. Twenty persons bore the image of the Virgin Mary with the Lord Jesus, adorned in the costliest manner, to the honour of the Lord God.

"In this procession very many delightful things were shown, most splendidly got up. Wagons were drawn along with masques upon ships and other structures. Among them was the company of the prophets in their order and scenes from the New Testament, such as the Annunciation, the Three Holy Kings riding on great camels and on other rare beasts, very well arranged; also how Our Lady fled to Egypt—very devout—and many other things, which for shortness I omit. At the end came a great dragon, which St. Margaret and her maidens led by a girdle; she was especially beautiful. Behind her came St. George with his squires, a very goodly knight in armour. In this host also rode boys and maidens most finely and splendidly dressed in the costumes of many lands, representing various saints. From beginning to end the procession lasted more than two hours before it was gone past our house. And so many things were there that I could never write them all in a book, so I let it well alone."

By the first quarter of the seventeenth century, religious bigotry, war, and economic strangulation had done their work. Dudley Carleton, writing in 1616, commented: "Antwerp I own surpasses all the towns I have seen in the magnificence of its buildings, the breadth of its streets, the strength and beauty of its fortifications. . . . Two sentences would suffice to describe the state of the place and you must accept them as literally true: *Magna civitas, magna solitudo*. For all the time I was there, I never could count in the whole length of any street more than forty persons at once. I saw neither carriages nor horsemen, and though it was a week-day, not one of us saw a pennyworth sold in the shops. Two porters and a ballad-monger could have carried off between them, all that was bought together in the Exchange, upstairs or down. The English factory was filled with scholars disciplined by the Jesuits; the House of the Osterlings [Hanseatic Merchants] stood empty. Grass grew in many of the streets. Curiously enough, in spite of its lonely state, the public buildings were well kept."

So many historical landmarks are gone that the city today is quite different from the one about which Guicciardini wrote and in which Plantin established his presses and Brueghel set up his easels. Even what remains of that period tends to be identified with later centuries—the Church of Saint James, for example, which is a mecca for tourists because Peter Paul Rubens worshiped there and is buried there.

The seventeenth century, the century of Rubens, was a time of reconstruction—mending, restoring, and in some cases rebuilding structures ravaged by conflict. The men of this century were good builders, and posterity owes a large debt to the artists who once more filled the churches and other buildings with paintings and sculpture; but their monuments, as lovely as some of them are, cannot really replace the lost treasures of the sixteenth century.

CHAPTER II

"What disputations there are"

THE Flemish and Brabant towns throughout the Middle Ages had a reputation for democracy. To Netherlanders democracy was a creed, a social force, a method of improving the life and material well-being and widening the spiritual horizon of the daily toiler. To them that government was best that could keep the greatest number of its people industrious, intelligent, comfortably housed, well clad, and economically prosperous. They also demanded a society that would provide pageantry, drama, music, and art works sufficient to satisfy the aesthetic tastes of all members of the community.

Democracy, which helped raise Antwerp to heights of glory, ironically contributed to the city's decline. Far too often liberty degenerated into license, and the word "Fleming" to outsiders was often synonymous with "revolutionary." Ultimately Antwerp, which had withstood political strife—indeed had profited from it—failed to bear up under the clash of religious opinions. As soon as Luther emerged on the historical scene, the city became factious. The poetess Anna Bijns wrote:

What disputations there are amongst people!
The world is full of error, where shall we flee

. . . .

Where have we come to! May God take pity on us.

Had she been able to foresee the future, she would have been even more distraught

Contrary to popular opinion, the religious struggle in the Low Countries was not merely one between Northern Protestants and Southern Catholics. Antwerp had undergone many religious and political tumults before Amsterdam agreed to the Alteratie in 1578, the expelling of a Catholic government and adoption of a moderate Calvinistic one. Because of its extensive economic ties, it was a gathering place for divergent beliefs. It was the natural center of the religious conflict.

As Professor Pieter Geyl and others have pointed out, however, it was military might that sealed the fate of Antwerp after 1585. The period between 1477 and 1585 began in revolt and ended in conquest. News of the death of Charles the Bold of Burgundy at Nancy (1477) was followed by popular uprisings in most of Brabant and Flanders. Mary, heir to Burgundy, was scarcely twenty years old, and the various town fathers saw a chance, with French help, to put an end to the steady encroachment of Burgundian power. In Antwerp a revolt known as the "Quaey Wereld" ("Evil World") broke out on March 17, 1477. The Town Hall was occupied, some private houses were invaded, and several magistrates were arrested. Some of the magistrates were illegally tortured by the rebels. Mary, for the moment, acquiesced and offered in the Great Privilege virtual automony for the Flemish cities. Her new husband, Maximilian of Hapsburg, however, punished the rebel leaders when he gained control, and Antwerp returned mainly to its former constitution, with rights going back at least to the first decade of the fourteenth century. These privileges had not been obtained by force, but, as Guicciardini pointed out, "by merit and by services rendered."

The different town halls of Antwerp during this period all bore insignias of the eagle and the Virgin, symbols that loomed large in Antwerp thinking. The eagle representing the Holy Roman emperor was paramount over the Virgin. The emperor exercised his ultimate authority through the duke of Brabant, who in turn delegated power to the margrave of the Holy Roman Empire. These last two offices by 1477 were synonymous, and the towns of Brabant had, since 1312 by a charter known as the Cortenburg, collectively exercised control over the duke by a council of nobles, commons, and clergy. It was the first institution of its kind in the Netherlands.

The dukes of Brabant and margraves of the Holy Roman Empire were Maximilian of Austria and Mary of Burgundy (1477–82), and Maximilian alone (1482–94). His son Philip the Fair was ruler (1496–1506), to be followed in turn by Charles V (1515–56) and Philip II (1556–89). Often, however, the office was filled by a regent: Margaret of Austria (1506–15 and 1518–30), Mary of Hungary (1532–55), Margaret of Parma (1559–67), Ferdinand Alvarez de Tolédo, duke of Alva (1567–73), Don Luis Requeséns (1573–76), Don Juan of Austria (1576–78), and Alexander Farnese, duke of Parma (1577–92).

The authority of the duke or margrave or his regent was exercised by the *schout* ("sheriff"), who represented the duke in criminal cases, and the *amman* ("bailiff") who was in charge of civil cases. The former made the arrests, acted as prosecutor before the magistrates sitting as judges in the *vierschare* ("court"), and carried out the sentence. The *amman* acted accordingly in his own sphere. Both officials had to be Brabanters and *poorters* ("freemen") of the city. Taxes were either due to the duke by customs or were negotiated between ruler and city.

In reality Antwerp was a free commune with a College of Magistrates having administrative, legislative, and judicial powers. The magistrates consisted of two burgomasters and, by 1558, eighteen *skepyns* ("aldermen"), a treasurer, a secretary, and an advocate. This group had jurisdiction and administration of the "freedom of Antwerp" and over the Scheldt from Rupelmonde to Zeeland. The burgomasters and the *skepyns* sitting in a set of four-tiered stone benches (*vierschare*) had power over life and death and at times took legal action against the duke and his representatives. They were even empowered to make treaties for the town without consultation with the duke.

They were advised by a broader legislative body, the Broad Council, which in addition to the magistrates included past *skepyns*, two *wijck-* or wardmasters from the twelve wards of the city, and two representatives (deans) from each of the twelve privileged guilds. A body of troops was commanded by the *schout*, but each ward had its own military under the jurisdiction of its *wijckmasters*. The military guilds, forces not under the *schout*, were all under the command of the chief burgomaster. For the most part, the rich burghers and noble families supplied the city with *schouts*, *amman*, and *skepyns*. Citizenship was easy to procure, and offered real protection by law. The foreign merchants in Antwerp had approximately the same liberties as the *poorters*, although they were not permitted to hold office.

Procurers controlled the weekly markets; almoners cared for the poor and the foundlings; and there were additional officials who decided petty trade disputes, officials for the police chamber, and syndics, who took cognizance of offenses against morality. All of these minor officials were selected by the magistrates. There also were many volunteer organizations within and without the guilds that carried on various civic duties, from welcoming the "Joyous Entry" of a duke into Antwerp to refurbishing a church, chapel, or public building.

Relief for the poor demonstrates how government and private citizens worked together. Some citizens—such as Jean van der Heyden, Gerard Rares, Herman van der Hoerke, and Dymphoe and Catherine Allaerts—left private houses and funds to provide for the poor and aged. Public relief was also available. Saint Elizabeth Guesthouse for old women, and institutions for the aged and insane were set up by the College of Almoners. That college consisted of four wealthy citizens who paid for the privilege of serving. The almoners supervised the four large public institutions, including the orphanages for boys and girls. They also were in charge of fourteen smaller houses. To refuse a position in the College of Almoners when selected made the individual liable to a hundred-florin fine.

A less powerful group of almoners was the "Table of the Holy Ghost," which controlled nine small hospices. Its main function was to distribute aid directly to the needy at the four parish churches: Our Lady, Saint James, Saint Andrews, and Saint Walburg. The officials of both the college and the table were responsible to the magistrates for the more than three thousand ducats spent annually on relief for the poor. Over eight thousand children were cared for and educated through public and private charitable foundations.

Unfortunately the Christian love that motivated these charities could not withstand the dogmas of the theologians, and the resulting deficiency of love stretched Antwerp on the rack of Reformation and counter-Reformation and made its sixteenth-century religious history a story of war, terror, and bigotry.

Antwerp had been beset by the heresy of Tanchelm in the Middle Ages, and at one time a group of Tanchelmians had controlled the town. The period before the Reformation had been one of deep piety, Antwerp having been a city of churches and religious foundations heavily endowed by the affluent populace. Still, the cosmopolitan qualities of the town undermined many traditions and customs that bordered on the superstitious, and materialism often caused the town to challenge ecclesiastical wealth, especially in land disputes. The idea that Antwerp embraced Calvinism to enjoy capitalism is rubbish. In Antwerp and its vicinity, Calvinism found its earliest supporters among the workers and small farmers. The large capitalistic families for the most part remained loyal to the Church or tried to steer a middle course.

This does not mean that they were oblivious to Protestantism. If war and diplomacy had not dictated otherwise, Antwerp might have followed Erasmus, who stressed faith and love over good works, and morality over relics. The religious searchings of many of those discussed in other chapters—Plantin and Brueghel, for example—were of men who placed personal piety over group worship, men who believed in the doctrines of the Brethren of Common Life and in the Family of Love. Many were pushed by the Inquisition into the camp of extreme Protestantism. Some became leaders in the Revolt against Spain. Some fled Antwerp to reside elsewhere—in England, Germany, and especially the Northern Netherlands. Others, weakened by defeat and degradation, made peace with authority, conforming outwardly but inwardly maintaining Erasmian ideas.

Antwerp was the focal point in the Netherlands' struggle with Spain. Events took place there which gave the revolt its distinct character, integrating complex religious, political, and economic issues. There passions reached their heights. The idea of Erasmus that mankind possessed in its reason a key to its own perfection was sacrificed on the altar of bigotry.

Even before Luther's Ninety-five Theses, a Flemish translation of the Bible had been printed in Antwerp (1516) by Nicolas de Grave, and the printing press was already spreading stories ranging from accounts of debauchery in the Papal Court to anti-Italian propaganda. A year earlier the magistrates had passed sentence on four men who openly ate meat on Ash Wednesday and who continued to do so in spite of reproof. Intellectuals and others resented the sale of indulgences.

Erasmus had appealed to the rational, to the learned, but only slightly to the masses. Not so Martin Luther. Lutheran ideas brought into Antwerp by German merchants blew the smoldering embers of dissent into flame. The first to take up Luther's cause were members of his own order. Two Antwerp Augustinians were burned for heresy at Brussels in 1523.

Two years earlier Charles V had issued his first placard against heretics. Luther's books were burned publicly. In 1522, Pope Adrian VI established a Commission of Inquisition for the Netherlands. This commission, acting on a series of edicts or placards, pronounced Draconic sentences on anyone even remotely connected with heresy. If the decrees had been carried out, every Netherlands town would have been clouded with faggot smoke. The first to suffer in Antwerp were Nicolas of 's-Hertogenbosch, a learned schoolmaster who was arrested and taken to Brussels, from whence he escaped, and Cornelis Graphaeus, secretary of Antwerp, who subsequently retracted his Lutheran beliefs. In 1522 the Augustinians were expelled from Antwerp. The prior Henry of Zutphen, already in jail for preaching outside of the priory, escaped to Germany. In 1525, Antwerp had its first religious execution: A monk was drowned for teaching Luther's doctrine. Three years later, as the placards became more severe, the first layman was put to death for religious opinions. The revolt initially had been Lutheran.

In 1535 the first Anabaptist, Jeronimus Pael, was executed, and ten years later the Netherlands' first Calvinist suffered a similar fate. By that time the Inquisition had become insatiable, and its demands were often resisted by the city magistrates.

The new creeds upset the authorities not only for religious reasons, but also because they bred lawlessness. Although some unrest could be attributed to social ills, most of it concerned religious doctrine. In 1525, Antwerp experienced its first round of image breaking, and in the same year Loy Pruijstinck, a slater, was preaching Loïsten doctrines to the wonderment of Catholic and Lutheran. The revolt became more radical. The Anabaptists renounced not only the Church but society as well. Their bizarre social and economic experiments at Münster turned both Catholic and Protestant against them. From this early group came most of the martyrs. The Antwerp Anabaptists were pietistic and had some appeal. Yet although they knew how to die with grace and dignity, they were not capable of rousing the people to resistance.

That task fell to the Calvinists. Based in Geneva and the

Walloon provinces, they began in the fifties and sixties to find a footing in the Flemish Netherlands. By 1554, François Pévuçel had established the first Calvinist congregation in Antwerp. The Calvinists gave the Reformation a new twist, seeking to reform the State. They succeeded because they had a highly developed political sense and because the international scene favored their cause. The Calvinists made preaching outside town gates popular, and soon their preachers in the fields were drawing thousands of listeners. The Baptists lost most of their followers to them, and inroads were made on the Lutherans.

Such was the situation when Charles V abdicated in 1555. The religious, political, and economic positions of the Hapsburgs had worsened steadily during the last years of his reign. Philip II, Charles's son, had the additional problem of being a foreigner. Almost at once he ran into opposition from both the nobility and the common people.

Space does not permit a detailed discussion of the causes of the Revolt of the Netherlands. National pride, customary liberties, and financial stability were all shattered by Philip II. The severity of the religious persecutions had alienated Catholic nobles such as Egmont and moderates such as William of Orange—not yet a Calvinist. The creation of new bishoprics such as Antwerp, although administratively justified, was politically stupid, conditions being what they were. The rebel nobility, mostly Protestant, assembled secretly and in 1566 presented a petition to the government. The scornful rejection of this petition from, as one official said, a group of "beggars" (*gueux*) constitutes one of the decisive events in Netherlands history. The term "beggar" became one of honor, and soon on land and sea *gueux* were taking, not asking. The ramparts of Catholicism began to crumble.

The regent Margaret worked to suppress the preachers, but it was like trying to stamp out a grass fire. Wherever an edict was proclaimed against preaching, the Calvinist consistory in Antwerp sent additional preachers. The more fiery the preacher, the more plaudits he received from his listeners.

As the summer progressed, Hendrik, count of Brederode, a rebel noble, with 150 followers clad in "beggars" gray, entered Antwerp to be received by a tumultuous populace as a liberator. Margaret, who distrusted William of Orange, sent him as burgrave of Antwerp (keeper of the fort) to preserve order.

Brederode withdrew, but a wave of image-breaking, starting August 14 at Poperinghe, swept the Netherlands. It reached Antwerp on the twentieth. What an orgy the looters had, and what a loss to Antwerp and world art! It was more than the destruction of images, decorations, carvings, and paintings. Jeweled chalices, crosses, patens, ciboria, candlesticks, vestments, and linens were also plundered. Harlots and "saints" drank consecrated wine from stolen cups. Money given for the poor was carried off; the organ of Our Lady's Church was wrecked. Even tombs were rifled for treasure. "These pillagers behaved not like Christian men but like Turks and Saracens." Music books worth hundreds of florins were destroyed. The damage was estimated at four hundred thousand crowns. The next day books were taken from monastic libraries and destroyed. It was open season on art, books, nuns, and monks. The Calvinists controlled the streets and the churches.

Orange was able to restore order, and an "accord" was passed August 23 promising to allow preaching if the people laid down their arms. Near the end of the year Calvinist forces defeated elsewhere moved in toward Brussels. Orange refused to aid them and remained at Antwerp while the Calvinists were cut to pieces at Oosterweel. Orange had hoped in vain for a compromise. He was not yet ready to throw his lot in with Calvinist radicals.

On August 22, 1567, Alva rode into Brussels. His 10 per cent tax crippled Antwerp's economy by its very existence and also because it drove non-Catholic merchants, foreign and native, from the city. Orange retired from Antwerp in October. A month earlier Anthony van Straelen, the city's chief burgomaster, was arrested and his property was seized; he was tortured and executed, dying faithful to Catholicism although an implacable foe of the Inquisition. He had tried to curb the image-breakers and at the time of the Iconoclasts had shielded Dominicans from the mob. Such acts of loyalty were overlooked. Alva had no use for moderates. The reign of blood and terror had begun. The decline of Antwerp and the crippling emigration started.

To overawe the town, Alva built a large military castle. Two thousand workmen were pressed into service—no doubt encouraged in their submission by the sight of gibbet and pillory. Four hundred thousand florins was levied on the town for its building—a sum approximately equal to the damage caused by the Iconoclasts. Alva advised Philip to delay a general pardon so that he could squeeze additional monies from those burghers threatened with legal proceedings. He also abolished the *vierschare*, depriving the citizens of all legal redress. Military rule predominated, with Frederic Perrenot, Seigneur de Champagney, the younger brother of Cardinal Granvelle, in charge. The rebels from North Holland, the "sea beggars," roamed the sea approaches. The town withered and endured extreme privation.

Requeséns, who succeeded Alva in November, 1573, was

more conciliatory. The *vierschare* was restored, but the people were plagued by the Spanish soldiers billeted in the castle. A general pardon was issued. Yet the city's commerce, by sea and by land, was crippled by the Revolt.

In 1574 only the presence of Requeséns prevented mutinous Spanish troops from pillaging and burning the town. Even then, citizens were held for ransom. Orange agents and fugitive Calvinist soldiers hiding in the city added to the menace.

Requeséns died March 5, 1576. After his death the troops of the States-General occupied Antwerp. Champagney was caught in the middle. He personally had prevented the troops of the States from killing the Spanish wounded, but could not prevent them from plundering the house of the Jesuits. On the other hand, he could not control his own troops, who were spoiling for a fight. They had been reinforced by mutineers from Aalst, who planned to obtain back pay from the civilian population.

On November 4, 1576, Spanish troops numbering about fifty-five hundred fell upon Antwerp, where there were eight thousand troops of the States and about twenty thousand *poorters* who could have fought. The people, however, were stunned to the point of paralysis—so much so that the "Spanish Fury" was allowed to run rampant.

People regardless of nationality were robbed and burned out, killed, or maimed. Poor people were often hanged because of their poverty, and the number of rapes and mutilations is unknown. The wealthy were often able to ransom their holdings (the Fugger factor paid eleven-thousand crowns). Eight thousand people were killed, and for weeks to come Antwerp was a nightmare peopled with Spanish soldiers. Dicing tables were set up in the Bourse, and it was hoodlums' and harlots' delight all around. What the Calvinist Iconoclasts had failed to destroy was wrecked by the Spaniards.

The disaster united Catholic and Protestant against Spanish rule. The Pacification of Ghent was signed, attempting to settle the religious question along regional lines. The Spanish soldiers left the city, and the castle was demolished. The Calvinists fought for exclusive dominion in many areas which they controlled, but where the majority of the population remained true to the old faith. They carried out a long series of violent persecutions against the Catholics, much to the chagrin of Orange and many of the moderates. The Amsterdam poet, Hendrik Spieghel, complained:

> *They who at first asked for no more than to live in freedom,*
> *Now have their liberty, but will not give it to others.*

During the so-called Religious Peace, the Catholics in Antwerp boasted that they outnumbered Protestants ten to one and that should there be trouble, they could count on Lutheran support. Yet in this same Antwerp a number of attacks which the government of Orange failed to control were made on Catholics. Catholic and Protestant unity was ruptured throughout the Netherlands. Antwerp joined the Protestant Union of Utrecht rather than the Catholic League of Arras. The city became the center of the Southern Netherlands' resistance to Spain. Attack after attack was made on it. Trade suffered, although the alliance with the rebels kept the sea lanes open. Many a burgher in his heart, however, found both Catholics and Protestants detestable. He wanted peace. Many emigrated in search of it.

One by one Catholic cults were eradicated. After the tide of battle outside the town shifted, the States-General in 1580 transferred itself to Holland. At the same time the Broad Council of Antwerp consented to invite the duke of Anjou to defend the city. Attempts were made to put the "Religious Peace" into operation. Anjou proved a weak reed, and the riot by French troops, the "French Fury," caused the death of eighty citizens. This time the citizens were better prepared, and 1,583 Frenchmen—a number equal to the year of the event—were killed, 250 being of high status. The "French Fury," however, cost Orange the confidence of the people of Antwerp. On July 22, 1583, he left the city, never to return.

Orange still controlled Antwerp, however. Philip van Marnix de St. Aldegonde, a loyal follower who was burgomaster of Antwerp from 1583 to 1585, was entrusted with the city's defense. Orange was assassinated June 10, 1584. In August of the same year, Parma began the siege of Antwerp, which fell to him after a heroic defense August 17, 1585. Thus Antwerp once more became a Spanish town.

Catholicism was reestablished, but the Reformed were given four years to depart. All privileges were restored, and no Spanish garrison was to be placed in the town. The castle was rebuilt but pulled down again after the subjugation of Holland and Zeeland.

Antwerp in 1585 was still, in spite of everything, the largest and wealthiest town in the Netherlands. But not for long. In Spanish hands the city was cut off from the sea first by military blockade and later by treaty. Its most able citizens continued to emigrate. Holland and Zeeland cities soon saw that it was better to leave Antwerp under Spanish control and bar it from the sea than to recapture it and have it compete against them economically.

CHAPTER III

"Venice outdone"

Accoding to Guicciardini, "Antwerp was the truly leading city in almost all things, but in commerce it headed all the cities of the world." Antwerp at its peak did more trade in a fortnight than Venice did in a year. "I was astonished and wondered much when I beheld Antwerp, for I saw Venice outdone," the Venetian envoy remarked. The exchange of merchandise was estimated at an annual average of 1.5 million florins. It was in Antwerp that Anthonie Fugger left his heirs 6 million gold crowns. In this city Gaspar Ducci entertained Charles V, and during the visit, threw a promissory note due him by the emperor into the fire. Similar stories are recorded of Jacob Fugger and another Antwerp moneylender. Fugger boasted that he had lent Charles V .5 million florins for his imperial election campaign in 1519, without which Charles would never have been emperor.

Antwerp between 1500 and 1575 was in the fullest sense a "Renaissance harbor." Its spirit of freedom was apparent in its attitude toward commerce: The city opened its doors to all. The harbor teemed with ships. Small by modern standards, they were vessels of the same kind that had carried Magellan and Columbus to the New World.

The economy of Antwerp boomed in the fourteenth, fifteenth, and sixteenth centuries. According to Dr. H. van der Wee, "It underwent the processes of rise, expansion, maturity, and decadence with peculiar intensity. . . . It was the heart of commerce, industry, and agriculture for a large area and particularly of Brabant, Flanders, and Zeeland. Moreover Antwerp's economy was an important, and sometimes even the principal, artery of the whole European economy."

Miss C. V. Wedgewood has expressed it thus: Antwerp was "a city which held a position such as [has] never been held before or since by any other town. For nearly a century . . . this cosmopolitan city controlled exclusively the money market of the known world, and the whole varied interchange of goods and wealth. Every nation had its concessions within the walls, every important loan in Europe was negotiated here."

During the crisis in Flanders after the death of Charles the Bold, Antwerp mostly remained loyal to Maximilian of Hapsburg. The grateful emperor rewarded the Antwerpians with a charter dated June 30, 1488, issued in his name and that of Philip, his son, the titular ruler of Antwerp. The charter ordained the transfer to Antwerp from Bruges of all the commerce of the Netherlands and invited the foreign merchants at Bruges to come to Antwerp, guaranteeing them the same privileges they had in that Flanders city. The next month Maximilian gave safe conducts and special protection to those merchants of Spain, the Hansa, Florence, Genoa, Lucca, and other nations who had come to Antwerp from Bruges, whose harbor facilities were rapidly deteriorating because of the silting of the Zwyn. Antwerp thus became the great port of northern Europe and the Low Countries, rivaled—but not closely—by Amsterdam.

The Antwerp fairs, which contributed so much to Antwerp's economic growth, permeated the life of the city.

Guicciardini waxed enthusiastic about "the two Martes that are in Andwerp, the one whereof, begynneth 15. daies before Whitsontide, and is thereof called La foire de Pentecoste. The other is called La foire de S. Remy or de S. Banan. because it beginneth the Second sunday after our Lady day in August, which is of equall distance from either of the saide Feastes. Each of these Martes endure six weeks, all the which time, no man is subject to any arrest for debt .... There are also at Andwerp besides these Martes, two great Horse faires: the One at Whitsontide, the other at our Lady day in September, and likewise two of Leather and skins of all sorts, which follow immediately after the horse faires."

The opening of the fair followed ancient and set customs. An official called Short Rod announced its opening in a house named the Maid of Antwerp, which was located on the Iron Bridge connecting High Street with the Market Place. On the morning of the appointed day the magistrates met at 9:30 at the Town Hall all clad in brown and black mantles—except the youngest, who wore crimson velvet. The latter chose a beauty to play the part of Maid of Antwerp. She was enthroned at her house and received the homage of the magistrates, to each of whom she presented a bouquet of red and white roses. The youngest *skepyn* was allowed a kiss, and gave her a plate of sugarplums. The *schout* declared the fair officially open, and the Short Rod took the Maid home by carriage. Throughout the six weeks of the fair, town minstrels played every night before the Town Hall.

During fair time, booths were raised all over the Great Market Place (the largest and most accessible open space in the city), in subsidiary marketplaces, and around the churchyards. The glove-sellers erected their stalls on the corner of the churchyard of Our Lady and today the Handschoenmarkt bears the name of the glove-sellers. It is here that the remarkable wellhead done by Quentin Massys still exists. In addition there were shoe markets, milk markets, linen markets, and others named for the traders who set up booths. South of the churchyard stood a pand for the exhibition and sale of pictures, statues, books, prints, and cabinet work. Many fairs featured pands, which were open spaces surrounded by covered galleries like the cloisters of monasteries. At one time it had been questioned whether it was proper to hold fairs on holy ground used for burying the dead, but the bishop of Cambrai ruled that such proceedings were in order so long as the stall-keepers did not sleep in the churchyard. Rents from booths and other profits no doubt influenced the bishop's decision.

The Horse Fairs were held in the Horse Market, an area lying between Klapdorp and Red Gate that still retains the name. Two fairs here lasted three days, one at Pentecost and one during Saint Bavo's Feast. Horses came in large numbers from all parts of the Netherlands and some from as far away as Denmark. Four days before each fair opened, the *amman*, with some solemnity and to the blowing of horns, declared all horses at the market and on their way thither to be under arrest from that moment on, so that it was not lawful to buy or sell them until the fair officially opened, the duke, his officers, and the magistrate excepted. Antwerp had a monopoly in the trade of horses, and the blacksmiths built a chapel on the Horse Market and dedicated it to Saint Giles.

The Cattle Market stood close by the Butcher's Hall, and the Hide and Skin Fair close to the Cattle Market attracted many people. The two hide fairs had earlier kept Antwerp going during a bleak financial period when all other staples had been removed to Mechlin. All sorts of hides were available, as were dried and salted meat and animal fat for eating and lubricating. Flemish immigrants from Antwerp with their frugal use of all parts of the animal carcass introduced oxtail soup into England. The Fish Market stood at the south of the burg partly inside and partly outside the city walls. Herring were smoked in a place called the Rookhuis ("Smokehouse") on the Kraaiwyk, where the boats unloaded fish from Holland and Zeeland. The Old Corn Market was close to the end of Brewer's Street, and grain brought from Zeeland apparently was sold at a market along the riverbank near Pieter Pots' Abbey.

The markets were usually open once a week, but during Antwerp's economic hegemony, markets and the fairs apparently ran continually. One market closed, another opened; one fair began as another dismantled its booths. Although the fairs laid the base for Antwerp's prosperity, the city's economy did not rest on a lone foundation.

William Jennings Bryan often stressed in his political campaigns that urban areas require a prosperous agricultural hinterland in order to flourish. Antwerp had just that. The Brabant countryside experienced as noticeable an economic revolution as did Antwerp itself. From 1496 to 1526 there had been a marked increase in the agricultural population and a decline in poverty. A decrease in grain production had been more than offset by the rise of an intensive type of farming. More cattle were being raised for dairies, and the urban boom had created a demand for such industrial crops as flax, hops, and oil. In addition, "turnip bread" and linseed-oil cakes were being used more and more for cattle fodder. The happy, prosperous peasants so vividly portrayed on the canvases of Pieter Brueghel supplemented their incomes by doing handwork at home for the growing linen industries. Later a decline in the demand for that handwork in the rural villages impoverished the people, and that blow, along with devastation of the countryside during the religious struggles, opened the ears of village handworkers to the social, spiritual, and economic messages of the Reformation.

Advances in agriculture are giant strides forward for all of civilization. Agricultural innovations made during the heyday of urban and rural Brabant changed the face not only of Brabant, but of Europe as well, especially England. The tremendous boom in truck gardening in seventeenth-century England and the Agricultural Revolution of the next century owe much to religious refugees from Flanders and Sir Richard Weston's *A Discourse of the Husbandrie Used in Brabant and Flanders*, published in 1650.

Row and bed cultivation, the growing of fodder crops on fallow land, increased use of fertilizers, commercial exploitation of forests, increased crop specialization, scientific stock breeding, pastoral and stable feeding of cattle, and the use of new crops and farm implements—ideas and procedures adopted by the English—were all customary practices of sixteenth-century Brabant horticulturists. English farmers began to experiment with two new crops, "great clover" and turnips, grown from Flemish seed, on land prepared by Flemish methods, with a "Dutch" plow to till the soil.

Dutch formal decorative gardens with their complex geometrical designs of paths and small raised beds of close-clipped hedges began to adorn the English landscape. Weston said that there were people in Surrey who knew "the first Gardeners that came into those parts, to plant *Cabbages* and *Cauliflower*, and to sow *Turnips*, *Carrots*, and *Parsnips*, to sow *Raith* (or early ripe) *Rape*, *Pease* and all which at that time were great rareties, we having few or none in *England*, but what came from *Holland* and *Flanders*." The result was a marked increase in rentals of plots of land and a change in the dietary habits of the ordinary Englishman. Brussels sprouts and salad greens appeared more and more on British tables.

From the Antwerp area, the Flemings introduced into the English gardens new types of herbs and flowers. Thomas Fuller, writing *The History of the Worthies of England*, commented: "The Dutch brought thither with them, not only their profitable craft, but pleasurable curiousities. They were the first who advanced the use and reputation of Flowers in this City (Norwich). A Flower is the best complexioned grass, (as a Pearl is the best colored clay) and daily it weareth God's Livery, for he cloatheth the Grass in the Field. . . . Great the Art in meliorating of flowers, and the Rose of Roses (Rosa Mundi) had its first being in this City. As Jacob used an ingenius invention to make Laban's cattle speckled or ring-straked, so much the skill in making Tulips feathered and veriegated, with stripes of divers colours."

Antwerp's economic revival, occurring about 1500, owed its initial impulses to structural changes in international trade. Navigation and commerce were taken over by new people. New trade routes developed. The transcontinental one had Germany as its base; another maritime route traversed the Atlantic. Antwerp was the focal point of these changes. The boom of English exports, the successful renewal of industry in the Low Countries, and the rise of the Antwerp Money Market were concurrent factors in Antwerp's commercial prosperity in the first half of the sixteenth century.

The larger Netherlands firms at first played a secondary

role. Such prosperous families as van Rechtergem, Schets, Pruynen, and Vleminckx, however, were involved in the copper trade derived from regional production for the Portuguese market. This group was an important link between Hungarian copper and Portuguese spices, but soon South German merchants acquired a monopoly in this trade as they did in the trade of the Brabant merchants based at the Frankfurt Fairs.

Italian merchants early in the sixteenth century lost their earlier firm footing in the Low Countries. Some important and well-established houses, however, still remained at Antwerp, headed by Gualterotti, the Frescobaldi, and the Affaitadi; but their weakening commercial position in Antwerp is forcibly illustrated by the bankruptcy of the Frescobaldi in 1518 and the liquidation of the Gualterotti in 1523. Spanish and Portuguese firms were mostly limited to the Crown spice monopoly, exploited primarily by the Portuguese.

Meanwhile the South Germans prospered. This was the age of their western European triumph, during which they assumed a commanding commercial lead. Their Antwerp houses became the terminal for the South German transcontinental trade. Huge fortunes were amassed. Between 1488 and 1522 the Imhofs increased their capital by 8¾ per cent per year on the average; the Welsers between 1502 and 1507 by 9 per cent; and the Fuggers between 1511 and 1527 by 54½ per cent. The amazing success of the South Germans is attributable to their industrial exploitation of copper, silver, and quicksilver, which could be immediately turned into capital, combined with a profitable long-distance trade based on the new commercial routes.

As the trade routes shifted, there were corresponding changes in organization in which more subtle methods of commercial exploitation were developed. As the monopolies grew, there was a renewed democratization of international trade in which large numbers of ordinary merchants participated. Increasingly, individual merchants—in spite of economic stumbling blocks—entered the lucrative trade that flourished between Antwerp and Seville, the Barbary Coast, the Canaries, Amsterdam, Danzig, and Riga.

Although big business flourished, there was a corresponding decline in corporate organizations. Sales of cloth, for example, were "concentrated either in the hands of local agents of important Antwerp firms or local or regional merchants who dealt independently with foreign or Antwerp firms." There was a remarkable expansion of "cash and carry" retail trade, and the price was "unaffected by the quantity purchased or the status of the buyer." Corporate buying by churches and other foundations decreased.

The Italians had introduced a "refined" commercial system by the fourteenth century. Antwerp, during the sixteenth century, developed new business forms and techniques based on earlier models. As was true in agriculture, there was an appreciable time lag between Antwerpian commercial innovations and their European adoption; consequently "their assimilation by the whole of Europe was a seventeenth century phenomenon."

Especially noteworthy were the rise of joint-stock companies and the practice of selling on commission. "The commission business made cheap buying and selling in distant markets possible, whereas the pooling of shares in a temporary company aimed at the successful financing of distant sea voyages." These two innovations allowed small merchants a fuller participation in long-distance trade and paved the way for later seventeenth-century practices.

Many changes took place in transport commerce. Smaller ships made more rapid transfers of goods and quicker turnovers. Convoys gave protection against pirates. Risks of loss were lessened by dividing merchandise among several ships. New processes in shipbuilding were tried, especially for the Baltic timber trade. Maritime insurance was expanded. Antwerp's superb port facilities were developed. All of these changes contributed to Antwerp's commercial success. At a time when Amsterdam could boast that five hundred vessels with grain and herring could be counted in its harbor, Antwerp could reply that almost as many came into that port on a single tide. As Miriam Beard in her *History of the Business Man* stated: "Perhaps never again will so great a proportion of the universal trade pass through a single harbor, or such an immense part of the world's credit-operations be transacted on a single exchange. Certainly, since Alexandrian times there had not been seen in the Old World so many products assembled from so many ports, dealt with in such amounts by companies so powerful and by men of such international orientation."

There was corresponding increase in overland transport facilities, which, although primarily originating in Hesse by people who drove the famous Hesse carts, aided Antwerp's transcontinental trade immeasurably, as did the organization of the sixteenth-century postal system. Over one thousand freight wagons a week came into the city from Germany, France, and the Low Countries to fill the shops of the merchants and to make Antwerp's daily market the busiest and richest in Europe. Changes were adopted in marketing organization and in the improvement of commercial techniques. The Brabant Fairs eventually became significant for the payment of commercial debts and for the transacting of financial business. In selling they were superseded by permanent sales halls such as the English House, the Hanseatic House, and so forth. The Tapestry-maker's Hall was another permanent sales center. Although Antwerp had developed no single goods exchange, a practice had grown up by the sixties—says Guicciardini—to carry on all commercial activity at noon and early evening in the "English Bourse," always one hour before the opening of the final exchange at the "New Bourse." This practice may be considered a forerunner of a permanent goods exchange, which was established in Amsterdam in the next century.

Italian double-entry bookkeeping was also adopted. During "the sixteenth century *mainly under the influence of Antwerp*, this technique was popularized and conquered commercial circles in Germany, the Low Countries, France, England, and even in the Hansa centers." In 1567 a John Weddington in Antwerp printed an English manual on the same subject. Improved techniques of payment, highly organized and active credit facilities, low interest rates, and the development of a system for discounting bills contributed to Antwerp's commerce during the city's heyday and to the economics of a more sophisticated Europe during the next century.

Antwerp's trade with England was one of the chief props for her economy, and so great was the traffic between the two countries that it represented nearly a third of Antwerp's marketing, as Guicciardini said, "in such sort that hardlye can they liue the one nation without the other." Some English contemporaries actually dated the beginnings of Antwerp's prosperity from the initial settlement of the English Wool Staple in Antwerp in 1338, which, of course, Antwerp writers vehemently denied.

When the Company of Merchant Adventurers came into existence in 1407, the merchants at first sent their goods to Bruges. Later they moved first to Middleburg and finally, in 1444, to Antwerp, where they received an extension of privileges. In Antwerp about this time the woolen cloth making changed to linen manufacturing; consequently, the city turned to England for woolens, many made by Flemish weavers or their descendants who had previously settled in England. The Adventurers sent twenty-nine thousand pieces of English cloth to the Antwerp Whitsuntide Fair of 1487 and "the prosperity of the Adventurer's Company dates from this period." The English were established in a trading house with cranes, weighing equipment, and storage space, and they lived close to the Bourse and the Market Place under their own civil laws. Eventually the sale of cloth outgrew the limited Fair time, and the stalls stayed open throughout the year.

This Anglo-Antwerp trade suffered many vicissitudes during the Wars of the Roses. After Bosworth Field, as Bacon points out, the Netherlands became "the sanctuary and receptacle of all traitors against the King [Henry VII]." Because Lambert Simnel and Perkin Warbeck were both backed by the Burgundian court, Henry VII withdrew the Merchant Adventurers from Antwerp in 1483 and set up a mart for English cloth at Calais. After an economic war which hurt both parties, Philip the Good of Burgundy and Henry VII agreed on February 24, 1496, to the *Intercursus Magnus*, which reopened the trade. The Netherlands promised neither to shelter nor to assist the rebellious subjects of Henry VII, and the Merchant Adventurers returned to Antwerp, where they were received by the delighted town magistrates with a great procession. Once more they were formally entrenched in their house on Wool Street. Matters still were not harmonious, and although several supplementary treaties and agreements became necessary, the *Intercursus Magnus* of 1496 remained the basis of all future agreements.

In 1501 the English merchants in Antwerp moved to Bergen-op-Zoom. The magistrates of Antwerp followed them there, begging them to return; and when they refused, all inhabitants of Antwerp were forbidden to do business with them or to go to Bergen-op-Zoom. In June, 1502, the differences were resolved and new advantages were granted to the English merchants who returned to Wool Street. Fresh troubles erupted in 1505 and soon became serious. The Venetian Vincenzo Quirini reckoned that the Antwerp Fairs yielded one-third fewer profits without the English. This 1505 dispute was settled, but it was followed by another quarrel in 1527 brought on by hostilities between Francis I of France and Henry VIII. Henry's marital problems also brought England and Antwerp into economic conflict. During these and subsequent disputes resulting from political differences, the English Staple settled at Calais, Middleburg, and Bergen. All such wrangling hurt not only the Exchange, but also the Antwerp workers who finished at least 95 per cent of the total English cloth goods that were imported. The final break between Spain and England sounded the knell to whatever Antwerp-English trade remained, and the Flemish cloth-finishers moved to England where they introduced the "New Draperies." To be sure, during the seventeenth century, English commercial relations with Antwerp were resumed, but by this time the path of remaining Anglo-Netherlands commerce was more likely to lead to the North Netherlands towns, especially Amsterdam.

Guicciardini has left a resplendent list of the articles and commodities exchanged by the English at Antwerp:

"Thence come Cloathes and Carsayes of all sorts and of them great abundance, both fine and course, Frises, fine wooll, excellent Saffron, but no great quantity, Tinne, Lead, Sheep skins, Cony Skins, and diuers sorts of fine furres, lether, Beere, Cheese and other victuals, and Malmesie brought out of Candia into England.

"Thither are sent Jewels, Pearles, and pretious stones, siluer vnwrought, Quick-siluer, Cloathes of gold and siluer, Silks, gold and siluer thread, Chemlets, Grograines, Turkyworkes, Spices, Drugs, Sugar, Cotten, Comin, Gaules, Linnen cloathes of all sorts fine and course, Sayes, Ruffels, Tapistrie, Madder, Hops, Glasse, poudered fish, all sorts of small wares, as well of metall as of other stuffe, Armor, all kinde of munition for the warres, and implements of house."

The most glamorous trade in Antwerp was in the exotic products of the Indies. Guicciardini tells us:

"The second cause of the wealth of Andwerp is this. In the year of 1503, the Portugales began to bring spices out of their Indias, and from Calicut into Portugale, and fro thence to Andwerp, which before that time were wont to be brought by the red sea to Barnt and thence to Alexandria, and so to Venice, which (before the Portugals voiage into the Indias) furnished all Christendome off spice. But the king of Portugale, having partly by love, partly by force, drawne all the traffique of spices in Calicut and Iles adiacent thereunto into his owne hands, and having brought them to Lisbonne, sent his factor with spice to Andwerp, by which meanes it drewe all Nations thyther to buy spices of the said Factor. Thus Andwerp by this occasion beginning to be greatly frequented: Afterwards in the yeare

1516 diuers Marchants strangers, Spaniards and Italians, departed from Bruges to go and dwell at Andwerp, and after them others, and so by little and little all strangers (a few excepted) left Bruges and went to Andwerp, with no lesse commodity to this citie, than discommodity to that."

Up to the sixteenth century this trade had been primarily in the hands of Hanseatic and Italian merchants. At the same time, the Spanish and the Portuguese were commercially active in the Netherlands, mainly out of Bruges. Events caused these two trades to merge. The decision of the king of Portugal to establish a factor, or agent, in Antwerp just six years after Portuguese sailors had rounded the Cape of Good Hope and three years after they returned from Calicut in Malabar did much to induce European merchants to move from Bruges to Antwerp. Antwerp, already open to the changing tides of international trade, moved quickly to capitalize on the situation. Nicholas van Rechtergem entered into a transaction with the Portuguese factor and was allowed to bring great quantities of spices by sea to Antwerp from Lisbon. From thence they were dispatched to Germany. Many other merchants, realizing how much expense could be avoided by bringing spices by sea—as opposed to the overland routes and the Venetian routes—entered enthusiastically into this venture. In 1505 the king of Portugal allowed Antwerp adventurers to purchase a great quantity of produce in the Indies and ship it straight to Antwerp in Portuguese ships. The houses of Fugger, Welser, Hochstetter, Imhof, Frescobaldi, Gualterotti, and Affaitadi shared in this enterprise and made huge profits. Eventually Antwerp merchants acquired from Portugal a monopoly on the Lisbon-Antwerp spice traffic. The Horse Fairs were the two great marts used during the spice trade.

English and Portuguese traders were primarily dependent on goods from Germany. The metals were bartered for colonial spices, and the Baltic products were exchanged for English woolens and Italian-Mediterranean luxury items. The Hanseatic League had moved its offices from Bruges to Antwerp in 1485 but went back there the same year. Four years later, however, they returned to Antwerp for good. From that time on, the trade with the Easterlings flourished in spite of war and bigotry. The house built for the Hansa was one of the impressive buildings in sixteenth-century Antwerp.

The Hanseatic trade had its center primarily in North Germany. From the Baltic lands came innumerable products, many basic necessities. After Amsterdam assumed the role of middleman between the Baltic and western Europe, that city's fortunes multiplied. Amsterdam's gain was Antwerp's loss, and already during the age of Guicciardini the North Holland ships, especially those of Amsterdam, were becoming more and more involved in the Baltic–west European carrying trade. The terminal, however, was still Antwerp.

The High or South Germans were even more important to Antwerp's commercial prosperity and its financial growth. Unlike the Hanseatic Germans, the High Germans did not constitute a single "nation" in Antwerp, but were separate groups from different cities with special privileges. They came from Augsburg, Ulm, Memling, Upper Bavaria, Franconia, and Hesse. These overland merchants had carried goods from Venice to Antwerp, but the fall of Constantinople endangered their position as the middleman between Venice and the north European cities. Other factors were significant also. Antwerp had far fewer disputes with the High German merchants than it did with those from England and the Hanseatic towns. Many of the High German merchants became citizens of Antwerp, leaving Germany and transferring the headquarters of their financial operations to the new Venice of the north. Antwerp, once a terminal, became the middleman, and Augsburg, once a middleman, became a terminal in the exotic spice transcontinental trade.

Among the most important High German firms operating in Antwerp were the Hochstetters out of Augsburg, who settled in the Hof van Berchem on the Lange Nieuwstraat, and the Fuggers from the same city, who initially exploited copper and silver mines in eastern Europe, then dominated the metals trade, and soon became paramount in finance. They could be found on the Steenhouwersvest Ijzeren Waag. Anthonie of this house left his heirs approximately six million gold crowns and backed the emperor Charles V in his war against the Schmalkaldic League. Also from Augsburg were the Welsers, who initially were in the silver trade but have the distinction of being the first major firm in the Lisbon–Antwerp–South German spice trade. This family occupied the "de Gulden Roos" on the Groentplaats. Anthony Tucher, who headed a firm of the same name and who established a money exchange at Antwerp, had previously been burgomaster of Nürnberg and the founder of a money exchange at Lyon. He rescued Antwerp's economic structure during the financial crises of 1557. A collateral member of the family, Lazarus Tucher, speculated in land, pepper, and other spices. In 1529 he was the government agent for financial affairs at the Antwerp Bourse, and one almost has to consider him an Antwerpian.

The trade with Italy remained an important cog in Antwerp's economy, but Antwerp, instead of being the terminal, became the center of the Italian-European trade. No longer did the luxury items of the Mediterranean and Italian world come over the Alps through Germany into Antwerp, but instead they were shipped via the sea routes to Antwerp and then transshipped into Germany. Goods from Antwerp were sent to Rome, Ancona, Mantona, Luques, Florence, Milan, Naples, Sicily, and Venice—the last city providing the most trade. To Rome, Antwerp exported cloth primarily. To Italy went English and Flemish cloth, such as sages, worsteds, linens, Arras lace, and so forth, to be exchanged for silks, satins, cottons, velvets, brocades, and other fine cloths produced in the Italian principalities. In addition Antwerp sent out spices—mainly from the Portuguese territories—household wares, tin, lead, madder, beeswax, leather, flax, soap, fish, cereals, metalwork, tapestries, and furniture. Even pepper was exported to Venice, the onetime pepper capital of Europe. From Italy came jewelry, drugs, gems, gum, cotton, some furs, "fine and curious workes," armor, wines, fruits such as oranges, and even Parmesan cheese.

French imports were primarily of bulk commodities, such as wine and salt. Each year forty thousand tons of wine, valued at about one million crowns, and sixty million tons of salt were shipped from French ports to Antwerp docks. France also sent forty thousand bales of woad (much in demand by Antwerp dyers), turpentine, pitch, writing paper, glasses, clothwork, and other merchandise, mostly small wares.

A large percentage of the imports, especially raw materials, was used in Antwerp's own industries, which ranged from cloth-finishing to making armaments. "Antwerp was the home of every luxury and industry that the genius of man could devise." Not the least of these industries was the book-publishing trade, so well represented by the House of

Plantin. Many of the city's citizens became extremely wealthy, "some here being worth 200,000 others up to 400,000 crowns a man, and more." These people, along with the master craftsmen and artisans, invested their money in commerce, building projects, and real estate. Thus they improved their economic status, so that "from day to day the city keeps on growing and flourishes, and increases marvelously."

Clothmaking and the finishing of cloth were the leading industries. It was here that the "new draperies" originated. Antwerp imported silkworms "contrary almost to nature and to the climate of this country," and its citizens produced and wove silk in limited quantities. Velvet, satin, damask, sarsenet, and taffeta were also manufactured, but a great deal of effort was expended in dyeing and finishing rough fabrics imported from England. Although the frenchified and italianate Englishmen may have been the style-setters in northern Europe, chances are that the actual clothing was made in Antwerp. This was especially true of ruffles, doublets, thread-stockings, lace handkerchiefs, and lace head-coverings. The Englishman John Johnson bought his mistress Sabine Saunders gay silken ribbons and "a neck-kerchief for my mistress" made of Antwerp bone-lace. For himself he bought three shirts at a time of fine lawn made at Antwerp, new shoes, new underhose to impress his lady, a lace-trimmed hat, new gloves, and perfume. He was especially taken with the satin and bombazine doublets, striped and enriched with gold and silver lace. Not only did the ruff come into England from Antwerp along with the use of starch, but it is also apparent that the spinning wheel was invented in Antwerp or nearby. A large number of refugee clothworkers settled in Norwich, and a goodly number could be found near Saint Katherine's

Ward close by the Tower in London. Most of these came from the Antwerp area. Thus Ben Jonson in *The Devil Is An Ass* alludes to this Flemish settlement, mostly Antwerpians:

> *To Shoreditch, Whitechapel and so to St. Katherine's,*
> *To drink with the Dutch there and take forth there*
> *patterns.*

Small wonder the distich:

> *Hops, Reformation, bays, and beer*
> *Came into England all in one year.*

There can be little doubt that all four were imported into Britain primarily by people who had lived at one time in Antwerp or its immediate vicinity.

The Val Saint Lambert crystalmakers of present-day Belgium stand in a long tradition of excellent Flemish glassmakers. Admittedly, Venetian glass was more delicate and lovelier than its Flemish rivals; nevertheless, Flemish glassblowers from the sixteenth to the eighteenth century dominated northern markets. Although heavier than its southern competitors, Antwerp glass was in great demand, and such Antwerp glassblowers as Casselair and Thomas Cavatto influenced London glassmaking in 1569. Also popular were Antwerp mirrors with highly elaborate frames; and many cathedrals in the Netherlands, England, and elsewhere remain a lasting tribute to Flemish workmanship in stained glass. The Antwerp Guild of Glaziers was one of the most famous in all Europe.

Not only glass but silver goblets were manufactured tastefully and in large quantities. John Johnson ordered twelve silver drinking pots for his wealthy landlord Sir Thomas Bridwell of London. "The pots would be with two ears each pot, and without cover, fashioned as ye know our English beer and ale pots be. The trenchers must be to lay a wooden trencher in the midst, as ye know the manner is, and about the round edge would be some pretty print or work." An excellent example of Antwerp's craft in gold and silver is the Founder's Cup presented to Emanuel College, Cambridge, by Sir Walter Mildmay and dated 1547.

Antwerp also did a flourishing business in beautifully embossed brasses to commemorate the dead and in brass and ironwork both useful and decorative. The wrought-iron decorative wellhead done by Quentin Massys in the Antwerp Handschoenmarkt is Antwerp ironwork at its best. Other fine examples were the fire irons, fire shovels, tongs, and fire screens in both iron and brass which decorated many north European homes. More useful than decorative were the cauldrons, hanging kettles, guns, armor, and even ovens—all made in Antwerp for outside purchasers. Loans to princes and the sale of armaments were often interrelated. As Guicciardini pointed out, the Belgians invented all sorts of "household stuffe, and instruments fit to make anythinge fine and handsome."

Antwerp pottery and tiles were sought after, but the Flemish genius expressed itself better in wood than in clay. Antwerp furniture can be seen in many of the paintings by Flemish masters, and some were considered priceless. The Flanders "Kist" was perhaps the most popular and outstanding piece of Flemish furniture. These chests were priced to fit the purses of all purchasers, and ranged from the ordinary variety covered with untanned leather and studded with brass nails to those covered with beautifully painted, stamped, and gilded leatherwork with silver ornamental nails fixed in such a position as to form intricate designs on the lid. Some were more substantially built and were bound with heavy but "charmingly" wrought iron bands and hinges. Nearly all of them had remarkably strong and exquisitely fashioned locks with even more elaborate keys. The Flemings were fine furniture-makers, and their peripatetic woodcarvers have left their imprints on chairs, choir stalls, pews, rood lofts, fonts and covers, angel beams, and church doors, not only in Antwerp and Flanders, but throughout Europe. There also was a large market for exquisite wooden dolls known as "Flanders' Babys."

The Saint Lucas Guild had in its membership over sixty different types of artists and craftsmen. Guicciardini said that there were in the city 169 master bakers, 78 butchers, 75 sellers of sea fish and 16 or 17 of freshwater fish; 110 barbers and surgeons; 594 tailors and bootmakers; 124 goldsmiths (not to mention a great number of cutters of jewels and other precious stones); and about 300 master painters and sculptors. Of shopkeepers, large and small, he said that the number was infinite.

The Bourse of Antwerp, which dominated European finance between 1515 and 1550, was the first real European financial exchange, and its importance cannot be over-estimated. A complete departure from the Flemish guild incorporations that had held sway in the Middle Ages, the Bourse was closely tied in with every important exchange in Europe. Guicciardini was enthusiastic about the straight discounting of bills and ordinary exchange, but took a dim view of those merchants who "impelled by avarice and insatiable thirst for extraordinary gain, have altered and corrupted this honest method of exchange." He was extremely unhappy over speculation in exchange rates and attempts of certain merchants to freeze funds, create monetary scarcities, and thus jack up interest rates. Except in periods of crisis, however, interest rates remained relatively low, and money could be borrowed there on the most favorable terms in Europe. Sir Thomas Gresham urged English merchants to make heavy deposits at the Bourse so that money would be plentiful enough for Queen Elizabeth to borrow at a low interest rate, and during the first three years of Elizabeth's reign, Gresham was able to obtain sums equivalent to well over five million pounds. Many loans went to governments who, in return for monies to fight their wars, gave the great bankers special privileges and monopolies. The heaviest borrowers were, of course, Charles V and his successor Philip II, but private individuals were also able to obtain considerable credit at the Bourse. When the relatively small Johnson Company went bankrupt, it owed its Antwerp creditors more than one thousand pounds. "Antwerp's contribution to banking technique in the sixteenth century . . . seems to have been considerable," van der Wee points out. "There is no doubt that the structural innovations there not only promoted discounting, but also laid the foundation of modern deposit and discount banking."

Antwerp played a significant role in the spread of bills of exchange. Discounting of bills developed in the city in the thirties. Much of the financial activity was carried on with comparatively little coined money. The merchants preferred the more convenient and safer method of giving and taking credit, the richer merchants often acting as bankers loaning money out at interest.

Jacob Fugger, who acceded to control of the family capital of two-hundred thousand florins in 1511, left assets worth two million to the firm when he died in 1525. He had advanced sizable amounts of money to Charles V, and his many loans to the emperor assured him of special favors,

as well as protection from his financial rivals, who wanted
to destroy him. This government and private banker con-
nection led to the tremendous expansion of credit operations in Antwerp, the small merchants investing money
with the great financiers so that they too might have a slice
of the pie. All of this helped bring about the price revolution in Europe and inflation. In fact, Antwerp probably had
as much to do with the rising price spiral as did the influx of
monies from the New World.

Behind the glittering economic façade, there were weak-
nesses. Military campaigns, the foreign policies of the
Hapsburgs, market fluctuations, and bad weather led often
to famines and hard times. By the middle of the century
the spice trade was almost entirely removed to Lisbon. The
wars of Charles V with France and the War of the Schmalkaldic League in Germany disrupted traditional trade and
trading routes. In 1557 the Spanish government transferred
its debts to state bonds at 5 per cent, and the Netherlands
government followed suit. Soon the French government
declared a moratorium on its debts, and in 1560 the Portuguese government declared bankruptcy. Europe's first
international bank crashed when Antwerp bankers were
unable to meet their obligations. As usual, the small investor
was the chief sufferer. This did not shatter Antwerp's
financial position, but it did weaken it. Trade fell off and
manufacturing slowed down as the money market de-
clined. The religious struggles, the ruinous economic policy
of Alva, and the rise of England and Amsterdam as exchanges added to Antwerp's economic troubles.

Antwerp's loss was London's and Amsterdam's gain.
There were many who favored England's assumption of
the Antwerp trade, but they disagreed about which city
should be the inheritor. At the time, entrenched interests,

especially in London, viewed Antwerp refugees with suspicion. One group said that geography had given the Low Countries their economic superiority and that their prosperity rested on wine taxes, so that "the beauty of Antwerp hath been maintained by drunkenness." Although the "Antwerp in England" plan came to naught, Antwerp's trade habits and practices, financial improvements—even its financiers, merchants, and artisans—did much to advance capitalism throughout northern Europe.

The city was like a great glowing hearth whose fires warmed and illuminated all those who came near it. Pirenne calls it a true city of the Renaissance. While Bruges clung to the old medieval ways and legislated to preserve them, Antwerp turned to the new age in deed and in spirit. It throve on the changing conditions and gave them its own unique twist. The first article in its constitution stated: "In this city all men are free and cannot be enslaved." The motto over the New Exchange read: "For the service of merchants of all nations and languages." Five thousand men gathered there daily, living proof of that dedication. One of the most interesting paintings in the Town Hall is a sixteenth-century scene showing the ceremonious naturalization of an Italian and his family, in which they are granted the freedom of the city. Loss of these freedoms, for natives and foreigners alike, helped bring about Antwerp's economic decline.

CHAPTER IV

"Arch-Typographer of the King"

N OT the least profitable business in the booming economy of Antwerp was the printing, sale, and distribution of books. Christophe Plantin, whose title was "Arch-Typographer of the King," worked at his trade in this Queen City of Netherlands printing. Of the 3,814 books that appeared in the Netherlands between 1500 and 1540, Antwerp produced 2,137, or 56 per cent. The city in the middle of the century had between 100,000 and 110,000 inhabitants, and there were about fifty known printshops during the first half of the century. It is estimated that approximately ninety-seven printers lived inside the city walls during that period. "The whole intellectual life of Europe . . . finds expression in the Antwerp printing press," one author claimed.

Printing had begun early in the towns situated in present-day Belgium. The first book in the South Netherlands was completed at Aalst in 1473 by Johannes de Westfalia and his partner Thierry (Dirk) Martins. The next year a press was set up in Louvain, and in successive years Bruges and Brussels followed suit. In 1480 there was a press at Oudenarde. Initially Bruges, in printing as in economics, forged ahead of other Brabant and Flemish cities. "It was really in this old Flemish town that the history of English printing began."

Mathias van der Goes published the first book in Antwerp in 1482, and from then on, the rise of printing paralleled the rise of the city. Van der Goes had, by the time of his death in 1491, produced 90 books. His widow married Godfrey Back, who carried on the business. Both van der Goes and Back were free masters of the Saint Lucas Guild, which had as members artists, engravers, printers, and painters. In his house (the Vogelhuis) on Brewers' Street, Back had produced no less than 160 works by the time of his death. He was one of the most active and most famous of the early printers in Antwerp.

Geeraard Leeu was the greatest Antwerp printer of the fifteenth century. Friend to Erasmus, he employed accomplished engravers, and as a result many of the engravings in his books were works of art. He came to Antwerp in 1484 and printed 147 books before his death in 1493. During his career, he had much to do with the printing of books in English, at least 7 of his publications being for English readers. A free master of the Saint Lucas Guild, he published in Latin, English, French, and Flemish, and his woodcuts illustrating old chronicles and romances of chivalry are delightful. He was without doubt the best typographer of his day, and his work far outshone that of his Antwerp rivals.

Just before his death Leeu brought to Antwerp the best printer in Belgium, Thierry Martins. This remarkable individual possessed a knowledge of Greek and Latin authors and printed their works along with religious tracts and writings by his friends Erasmus and Sir Thomas More. Between 1500 and 1539, he produced some eighty-five editions of such authors as Rudolphus Agricola, Erasmus, Pico de la Mirandola, Angelo Poliziano, Jacques de Middelbourg, and Gregory the Great.

It is difficult to identify definitely many of the early

Antwerp printers, because they had a habit of borrowing and lending each other materials. Identification becomes increasingly complicated for books printed after the religious squabbles broke out, because many printers went underground and used fictitious names and colophons. Nicolas de Grave in 1516 issued the first Flemish Bible printed in Antwerp and followed it with another in 1518. Michel Hillen van Hoochstraaten was the most productive of all the pre-Plantin printers. By 1540 he had published 493 books. Most of his editions were from the pens of famous Netherlandish humanists, such as Erasmus, Johannes Graphaeus, Barlandus, Latomus, and others. His daughter married Johannes Steelsius, who printed in Latin, Netherlands, French, and Spanish. Steelsius's output included not only Bibles and religious tracts, but also texts by scholastics, humanists, and contemporary "literary" writers. Willem Vorsterman between 1505 and 1540 printed 286 books with woodcut illustrations. Another Antwerp printer, Martinus de Keyser, published much material for the English book trade—for the most part anonymously—and apparently avoided the authorities by publishing Catholic works at home and Protestant tracts for England. Among his orthodox English works were two editions of John Colet's *Aeditio*.

The religious struggles gave a decided impetus and a new theme to printing. The warring religious camps employed printers to spread their ideas, and the result was a tremendous increase in the quantity of publications, although the quality often was low. Early in the sixteenth century, the decrees of the Church against seditious books and pamphlets caused some printers to become extremely cautious. Others, motivated by religious zeal or secular greed, sometimes tossed caution to the winds and became victims of their own rashness.

Some were true martyrs to the cause of freedom of the press. A small batch of forbidden books was found in the shop of Adriaen van Berghen, and he was put into the city prison, the Steen. After a long spell of confinement during a lengthy trial, he was ordered to leave Antwerp and make a pilgrimage to Cyprus. An even more famous case was that of Jacob van Liesveldt. Born at Antwerp about the turn of the century, Liesveldt brought out his first book in 1536. He spent a good portion of his remaining years publishing religious works—especially the Bible—in the vernacular. His first edited version appeared in 1526 and by 1542 had gone through six editions. His work is the first complete Bible in the Netherlands language, and is based primarily upon Luther's German translation. This "Liesveldtsche Bÿbel" influenced the subsequent development of the Dutch language and literature; preferred by Belgian Lutherans, it was read throughout the Low Countries. Calvinists and Mennonites also used it. As late as 1620, a bookdealer in Protestant Hoorn grandly displayed a signboard for his shop with the proud title "In de Liesveldtsche Bÿbel."

Needless to say, Liesveldt's activities soon brought him to the attention of anti-Protestant forces in the government. In 1536 the magistrates of Antwerp were ordered by the central government at Brussels to burn the Bible and other works published by Liesveldt. In 1542 he was arrested for issuing a religious tract taken from the Germans. He acquitted himself of this charge by pleading that never before had he been forbidden to publish extracts of books. The work, however, appeared at a later date on an index of prohibited books published by Plantin. In 1545 he once more came into conflict with the authorities by bringing out an edition of the Bible with marginal notes affirming that Christ was the sole way to salvation. He again pled not guilty and said that an identical Bible earlier had been printed under privilege. This time, however, his position was more serious, and his defense faltered. He was beheaded on November 28, 1545. His wife continued his policies and suffered the same fate a year later.

Liesveldt did not limit his output to Protestant works. In 1528 he published the famous *Refereinen*, the first book of poems by the Catholic poetess Anna Bijns. He also brought out in 1544 a New Testament in French by Sir G. van Havra. His son, Hans, who succeeded him, published, among other things, a translation of Vergil's *Aeneid* by Corneille van Ghistile (1554).

English Bibles were also edited and published in Antwerp. Although a few sheets of William Tyndale's New Testament were printed at Cologne and two editions of it were brought out at Worms, a half-dozen more editions were done at Antwerp before the translation was allowed to appear in England. Jacob van Meteren, the father of the historian Emmanuel, was a wealthy Antwerp merchant who frequently had business in London. A zealous and pious Protestant who wanted to advance God's work in England, van Meteren took Miles Coverdale into his service to do an English translation of the Bible. Like Erasmus, who wanted the laboring ploughboy to sing the Psalms, van Meteren was more interested in utility than in a scholarly version based on the original Greek and Hebrew Scriptures. In fact Coverdale, who now resided in Antwerp, would not have been capable of such an undertaking. Consequently, his edition was drawn from the Latin Vulgate and an earlier Dutch translation. Van Meteren out of his own pocket paid for having the full work printed. His purpose was, as he said, "tot groote bevordering van het Rijche in Engelandt." The Coverdale version of the Bible appeared in 1535. In 1538 his New Testament was brought out in Antwerp by Guihelmus Montanus.

Tyndale came to Antwerp to complete work on his Old Testament, and it was there that he was eventually arrested and turned over to the authorities for execution at Vilvoorde. John Rogers (1500?–55), the first martyr of the Marian Persecution, met Tyndale in Antwerp and deserted the Roman faith. Before being arrested, Tyndale gave his unfinished work to Rogers, and Rogers spent the year 1536 preparing for the press an English version of the complete Bible. He added the work of Coverdale to his own and Tyndale's, and the whole was printed on van Meteren's press. Richard Grafton of London purchased the printed sheets, gave Archbishop Cranmer a copy in July, 1537, and subsequently received permission to sell the entire edition of fifteen hundred copies. A second edition in 1538 is noteworthy for its prefatory matter and marginal notes that constitute the first English commentary on the Bible.

The presses of Antwerp did not serve the cause of Protestantism exclusively. Antwerp from the beginning of the Reformation was the headquarters for Roman propagandistic literature directed at England. John Fowler had a most active Catholic press in the city. From the end of the sixteenth century onward, Antwerp became the center of the counter-Reformation. When Antwerp booksellers were no longer able to issue Protestant tracts, they flourished by printing Bibles, missals, and polemics for the Catholic market.

Over and above all other printers and bookdealers tow-
ered the House of Plantin-Moretus. Guicciardini said of
De Gulden Passer ("the Golden Compasses"): "This magnificent printing house [was] established next to the shop,
and a particular house all belonging to Christopher Plantin,
printer of the King; whose enterprise is worthy of our
praise and remembrance; in so far as such an establishment
has never been seen, nor is yet seen in the whole of Europe,
with more presses, with more type of various kinds, with
more prints and other instruments, appertaining to so excellent an art; with more capable and competent printer's
assistants, earning higher wages by working, correcting and
revising in all languages, strange as well as familiar, none
excepted, which are used throughout the whole of Christendom."

This world-famous establishment steered an intellectual
but stormy course through war and censorship, image-
breaking and bigotry, siege and sacking, royal displeasure
and royal favor. It achieved its greatest success under its
founder, Christophe Plantin, but its most famous and splendidly done books—save one—were printed by his grandson,
Balthasar I Moretus, who was a schoolmate and close friend
of Peter Paul Rubens.

Although Plantin was not a native of the city, having
been born about 1514 at Saint-Avertin, which is near Tours
in France, he picked Antwerp "above all other towns"
when, already an accomplished printer, he left Paris in
1548, at which time Henry II of France, in his zeal to crush
heresy, was making practice of the printer's art extremely
dangerous. When Plantin arrived in Antwerp in 1549, it
was already one of the great centers of the printing world.
On March 21, 1550, he went through the formal and
elaborate ceremony of becoming a citizen of the city, and

the same year, was made a member of the Saint Lucas Guild. From that time on, with few exceptions, his career is inextricably entertwined with the history of his adopted city.

At first he did not work as a printer, but opened a shop where he sold prints and books and his wife sold haberdashery. He also bound books and decorated leather and other jewel boxes. Soon he became recognized as one of Antwerp's most skillful leatherworkers and bookbinders. In 1555 he was in the process of delivering a richly wrought leather case to Gabriel de Çayas, secretary to Philip II. As he crossed the Mier at twilight, some drunken hoodlums mistook him for a guitar player against whom they had a grudge. They attacked the unfortunate Plantin, stabbed him in the shoulder, and nearly killed him. On recovery he was unable to handle gilding tools and consequently gave up bookbinding for printing, to the great profit of scholarship and bookmaking.

The firm was a family affair. Plantin's younger daughters, even before they were twelve years old, were required to learn to read handwriting and to serve as copyholders, often for books written in foreign languages. Sons-in-law Francis Raphelengius and Jan Moretus worked as correctors—reading, editing, translating, rewriting, and preparing copy. Raphelengius later (1585) ran the branch of the firm in Leiden, and Moretus was Plantin's chief clerk and successor, and father of Balthasar I. Another son-in-law, Gilles Beys, was director of a Plantin book agency in Paris, and Plantin's wife and daughters operated a small bookstore in the cloisters of the Antwerp Cathedral.

Balthasar III Moretus in 1692 became the first printer to be knighted, and the firm continued to operate under the control of the family until 1876, when its buildings and grounds were purchased by the town fathers of Antwerp. At that time De Gulden Passer passed from a working printshop to a city museum—one of the world's unique museums.

Plantin's first book, social and moral instructions for a girl of noble family, was printed in Italian and French the year he was stabbed, and his reputation as a printer-publisher was firmly established in 1559, when he issued a splendid book describing and illustrating the funeral ceremonies in Brussels of Charles V.

All did not run smoothly, however. In 1562, Plantin was accused of having printed a heretical book. Three of his assistants were arrested, but he avoided prison by taking refuge in Paris. While he was there, his creditors sold his furniture, but apparently they did this so that it would not be confiscated. One of these "heartless creditors," Cornelis van Bomberghe, renewed a close friendship with Plantin on the printer's return in 1563 and, with his nephew Charles, entered into a partnership with him. Other partners in the company were Jacob de Schotti and the physician Goropius Gekanus. Plantin became technical manager and director, the others being merely financial backers.

The new company was successful from the very beginning. During the five years it existed, 260 works were published. Seven presses and forty workmen were employed in the business, and it was during this period that Plantin became recognized as the foremost printer in the world. He maintained friendly relations with the city authorities—indeed, Antwerp gave him special privileges—and carried on a wide correspondence with scholars and artists. Although rulers such as the king of France and the duke of Savoy offered him monetary reward to set up printing establishments in Paris and Turin, he preferred to stay in Antwerp.

He increased the quality as well as the quantity of his publications. Pocket-sized editions by classical authors containing commentaries by learned men such as the Antwerpian Theodore Poelman appeared in many libraries. The Plantin Hebrew Bibles were sold as far away as Morocco. Other well-put-together liturgical works were published, as were the richly illustrated anatomical dissertations of Andrew Vesalius.

In 1570, at the peak of his prosperity, Plantin received from Philip II the title *Prototypographus regius*. "Arch-Typographer of the King" was an honorary position, but Plantin accepted it with certain reluctance and reservations because it meant that he personally had to observe all printing ordinances in addition to supervising his colleagues. Although this thankless and unpaid task lost its significance when the struggle broke out against Spain, it did give Plantin and his successors a certain distinction and a monopoly on the sale of certain liturgical works in Spain and the Spanish colonies. During Plantin's life this monopoly was not very important, but in subsequent generations, it helped the firm through difficult times. From 1572 on, the House of Plantin-Moretus sent thousands and tens of thousands of missals, breviaries, diurnals, antiphonaries, and psalm books to Philip II and his successors, who sold and distributed them throughout the vast Spanish empire. All of these items were masterpieces of their kind and sold just as well outside Spain and the colonies.

Prosperity made Plantin more conservative. Despite the ebb and flow of events, he remained outwardly a member of the Roman faith; and although he claimed that the questionable orthodoxy of his partners was the reason for a rupture which occurred in the company, he always had a strain of unorthodoxy in his own spiritual makeup. The two Bomberghes and Schotti, shortly after falling out with Plantin, fled from the Inquisition because of their Calvinist faith, and Plantin appeared to loosen his ties with Calvinism and the Family of Love doctrine proclaimed by Henry Niclaes, with whom he had been closely associated since 1549, and whose works were printed with type loaned by Plantin to Niclaes's publisher, Augustin de Hasselt. In the years following the Spanish Fury, Plantin remained close to Henry Jansen Barrefeld (Hiël), a religious reformer who, without leaving the Catholic Church, had revealed a number of heterodox opinions in several writings that Plantin printed.

Religious publications could not completely contain or limit Plantin's tremendous energy. Now sole owner of his company, he found the necessary time, capital, and opportunity to publish some of the best scientific and learned works of his time. Among these were several handbooks on botany by Dodoens, Clusius, and Lobelius, and the *Thesaurus Theutonicae, lingae*, the first dictionary of the Dutch language, compiled on Plantin's own initiative. Many other books followed in these, the flourishing years, of Plantin's career. It is well to note that at no time in this period did he operate less than sixteen presses. At one time twenty-two presses were in use and two hundred gold crowns daily was required to pay the salaried workers. At the same time, the Estiennes, the greatest French printing family of the sixteenth century, never used more than four presses.

In this period Plantin conceived his plan for a complete scientific and reliable edition of the Biblical text. Through the intervention of de Çayas and Cardinal Granvelle, Plantin was able to interest Philip in his ambitious scheme. The Spanish king promised financial aid and sent his chaplain, the great humanist Benedictus Arias Montanus, to act as scientific adviser. Raphelengius, a renowned specialist in Oriental languages, also rendered valuable service.

The printing began in 1568 and was finished in 1572. It cost the staggering sum of one hundred thousand florins to issue twelve hundred copies. The *Biblia regia*, or *Biblia polyglotta*, is in five languages—Latin, Greek, Hebrew, Syriac, and Chaldean. In addition it has detailed appendices which include Hebrew, Chaldaic, Syrian, and Greek grammars and vocabularies, along with studies on the measures, costumes, and habits of the ancient Hebrews. The book is filled with full-page illustrations made from copper plates. "It consisted of eight big in-folios, was Plantin's masterpiece, and is the most important work ever produced in the Netherlands by one printer."

The work earned more honor than profit. Indeed, the printing of the Polyglot Bible was the beginning of financial troubles from which Plantin never completely recovered. The king was negligent in his payment of subsidies which amounted finally to six thousand ducats, for which he was to receive an equal value in books at trade rates. The more expensive volumes cost two hundred florins a set, and the less elaborate ones sold for seventy florins a set, an extremely high price for those times. The king in addition ordered twelve copies in vellum, which required more skins than could be found in Antwerp or Holland. Plantin himself did not like vellum and refused to do a copy in it for a German prince, saying that copies on imperial Italian paper were better printed than those on vellum.

Clearing the books for sale was a nearly insurmountable problem. In spite of royal patronage, Philip II would not allow the work to be published without papal approval. Montanus himself went to Rome to persuade the reluctant pope to allow publication, but it was not until 1573 when a new pope was in the chair that the permit was obtained. More troubles followed. A Spanish theologian denounced the work as "heretical, judaistic, the product of the enemies of the church." The Inquisition examined the work laboriously "and grudgingly decided in 1580 that it might be lawfully sold." During the seven years that the orthodoxy of the book was questioned, Plantin suffered financially because much of his capital was frozen. Before printing the concluding volumes, he had to mortgage, at nominal prices, two-thirds of the copies already printed. Philip refused to help with an outright subsidy but did grant Plantin an annual pension of four hundred florins gained from a confiscated Dutch estate, "but the perverse Dutchman who owned the estate soon retook it." Plantin's financial sacrifices, however, benefited the intellectual, scholarly, and book worlds.

Inevitably, most of the great printing houses were soon entangled in the religious conflict. Although Plantin's plant escaped destruction from the Spanish Fury in 1576, and was not plundered, production was slowed down considerably. Furthermore, as the printer said, "Nine times did I have to pay ransom to save my property from destruction; it would have been cheaper to have abandoned it."

By 1577 only five presses were at work. Later on, this number was sometimes increased, but never again did the great printing house operate more than ten presses. During these bleak times Plantin had to cope with a king who could neither pay his debts nor keep order in the city, creditors who did not trust him, and lack of customers, since few dared come to the strife-ridden city. Aging and tired,

Plantin worked away at paying his debts. He often sold at ridiculously low prices some of the rare books he had so painstakingly collected. At times he was forced to part with some of his working tools. In 1581 he went to Paris and disposed of the remainder of his library for sixteen thousand francs, less than half its true value.

In the turbulent times through which he lived, Plantin in the precarious trade of printer accomplished phenomenal feats of legerdemain. While the Spanish troops of the infamous duke of Alva occupied the Southern Netherlands, Plantin under orders printed a placard entitled *Catalog of Prohibitive Books*. Two on that list had been previously published by Plantin himself—the *Colloquies* of Erasmus and the *Psalms* of Clement Marot. After the Spanish Fury, Antwerp lined itself up on the side of the rebels. This placed Plantin in a difficult position. Again he tacked against the winds of partisanship. He published several anti-Spanish works without openly defying Philip. At the same time the astute "Arch-Typographer of the King" not only obtained the favor of such rebel princes as William of Orange, the archduke Matthias, and the duke of Anjou, but in addition became the official printer for the States-General, the leading political body behind the revolt. He was concurrently the official printer for Antwerp.

During 1583, when the troops of the duke of Parma threatened the city from without, Plantin, with the consent of his creditors, temporarily transferred his printing office to his sons-in-law and went to Leiden to accept a position as printer for the newly erected unversity there. His salary was two hundred florins, and he stayed for three years. Although he was a Roman Catholic in a Calvinist stronghold, he was treated cordially. He left in August, 1585, planning to go to Cologne. On learning that Antwerp had fallen to the forces of Alexander Farnese, however, he returned to his adopted town, where he continued to print and publish until his death on July 1, 1589. He died in the Roman faith and was buried in the round gallery of the high choir of Our Lady's Cathedral in Antwerp. His successors, the Moretuses (Moerentorps), who through Plantin's daughter succeeded to the business, were orthodox in their religious beliefs, but no less liberal than Plantin in what they printed.

During Plantin's thirty-four years in Antwerp, through good times and bad, he published more than fifteen hundred works, nearly an average of fifty a year. This was a phenomenal record for that time, and it made Plantin the first great, and for a long time unrivaled, "industrial printer" in Europe.

It is as an industrial printer that he is best remembered, but a look into the operation of his shop provides an insight into Renaissance printing itself. After the death of the founder, the number of presses used by the firm varied from five to ten. At his death an inventory showed that he had seventy-three fonts of type weighing 38,121 pounds. Plantin had his own type foundry, but like every eminent printer of the sixteenth century, he had some custom-made types which he alone used. Although he hired Henrik van der Keere of Ghent to make type for him, the greater part of his equipment was made by Frenchmen. At first other printers like Plantin probably hired an engraver to draw and cut in steel the model letters, or punches, and to provide the accompanying molds and matrices. The punches belonged to the printer, who took them to the type founders, who furnished him with all the type he needed. Two Antwerpians cast Plantin's early types—Guyot and van Everbrocht. After 1563 the type was cast in an office designed for that purpose, but type-casting was not a large part of the Plantin-Moretus printing establishment until after 1563.

Plantin excelled in the use of Roman type. Johannes de Westfalia brought this type from Italy in 1471 and appears to have been the only Low Country printer who used it during the fifteenth century, but it was not used really well until 1555, when Plantin established his press at Antwerp. Plantin and, after him, the Elzevirs of Leiden and Amsterdam were "destined to eclipse all other artists in their execution of this letter, which in their hands became a model for the typography of all civilizations."

The Plantin account books state that he paid forty-five florins for copper platens for six of his presses, just five florins less than he paid for a font of type. That he used platens is an unexpected discovery, showing that Plantin knew the value of a hard impression surface and made use of it three centuries before it became generally adopted by the printing world.

Paper was easy to obtain because Antwerp was a European distribution center for it. Plantin used paper from Italy, Germany, and France, but preferred French paper, for which he paid between twenty-four and seventy-eight sous a ream. Vellum skins came from Holland at the price of forty-five sous a dozen. Many Englishmen, such as the Johnson family, bought "Fine Lyons" in Antwerp as well as their inks. Plantin paid various prices to his binders. A full sheepskin binding in quarto form cost one sou a copy. A folio in full calf might bring a binder seven or eight sous, and richly gilded copies were appreciably higher.

Much of Plantin's success rested upon efficient management. Although he paid his employees relatively small salaries and held them strictly accountable for their work, he nevertheless had loyal workmen. Furthermore, he often

helped former employees set up their own printing establishments, although he preferred them to go outside of
Antwerp and the Southern Netherlands. The average
yearly wages of expert compositors were 142 florins a year,
and pressmen were paid 40 florins less. Work began at 5:00
A.M., but no quitting time is stated in the labor contracts.
It can be assumed, however, that the men worked until
dusk. Within the press and composition rooms discussions
on religion were prohibited, and compositors who set three
words or six letters incorrectly were liable to fines. Every
workman paid for his entrance into the Plantin organization with a *bien venue* of eight sous as drink money and
contributed two sous to the poor box. At the end of each
month the poor box received thirty sous and the *bien venue*
ten.

In the Correctors' Room of the Plantin Museum is a
painting by Pieter van der Borcht (1540–1640) entitled
De Proeflezer ("The Proofreader"). This painting, supposedly of Cornelis Kiel, shows a benched, bearded scholar
clad in a leather bluish tunic and long socked pants, bending
over manuscripts with a single eyepiece. From the painting
one actually senses dedication to excellence, which Plantin's
proofreaders must have had, and an appreciation of the
arduousness of their task.

In 1575, besides his two sons-in-law Francis Raphelengius
and Jan Moretus, Plantin employed five other correctors
for his twenty-four compositors, thirty-nine pressmen, and
four apprentices. In spite of the fact that Plantin held his
proofreaders accountable for errors and fined them on a
scale against their daily wage, the work was not very well
done. The *Royal Polyglot*, for example, had 115 errors of
paging in the eight folio volumes. "Yet this work was

supervised by Montanus, Raphelenguis, and in some portions by eminent scholars and professors of Leiden University." Cornelis Kiel was perhaps the most competent of the Plantin editor-proofreaders. Plantin persuaded the thirty-year-old Kiel to come to Antwerp from Louvain. Kiel probably had studied at the university there, and had worked in a printshop. Plantin wrote in his day book: "On Sunday 6 March 1558 Cornelis came here to dwell in the establishment and for his work will receive twelve stuivers per week plus room and board." Kiel supervised the proofs and was paid an additional sum for all extra tasks. He lost his place when Plantin closed in 1562, but when he reopened in 1563, Kiel rejoined him. He did not, however, come to live in Plantin House until June 24, 1565. He was to be paid four florins a month for the time he was proof-reader, and it was stipulated that he would read proof only for the more accurate pressmen and typesetters. A later contract regulated his salary according to the number of presses in operation. It should be noted that Kiel received 75 florins a year, whereas the best printers received 150, and the carpenter who lived in received about 250. In September, 1580, however, he received 12 extra florins for correcting the *Kruidboek* of Lobelius. He also obtained money from interests on loans to Plantin and for back pay. Kiel's intellectual accomplishments will be discussed later.

Raphelengius, afterward a teacher of Greek and Oriental languages at the University of Leiden, received forty florins a week plus room and board. The highest salary he attained was four hundred florins in 1581. Lower on the scale, scholars like Ghisbrecht worked for a mere pittance, considering their knowledge. The world-famous philologist and humanist Justus Lipsius appears to be the sole scholar outside the family adequately paid for his literary work, and he, of course, was one of the closest friends of the great printer.

Authors fared little better than scholarly proofreader-editors like Kiel. As a rule they were paid off in books. At times they received ten florins for the manuscript of a salable and valuable book. As is now sometimes the case, authors and editors contributed to the cost of having their works printed. Plantin in a letter to Jacques Strade, October 10, 1578, said that he was not in the habit of selling books at a discount to authors, but if he published an author's work, he gave him one or two dozen copies of it.

Plantin's editions were relatively large for that time, ordinarily numbering 1,250 copies. The largest edition he ever printed was 3,900 copies of the Pentateuch in the Hebrew. He refused to contract or print small editions unless he was paid the cost of production in advance.

He sold very few single copies, confining himself primarily to the wholesale trade. He gave his wife and daughters a small discount amounting to about one-sixteenth of the retail price on stock for their bookstore. His wholesale prices varied from an eleven-sheet edition octavo of Horace for one sou to the Polyglot in eighty volumes for seventy florins, about $140. A single copy of a Bible in Latin cost one florin.

Plantin was not an ordinary peddler of books. Admittedly many of his books are not of the highest quality, either in format or presswork, and there were obscure rivals in France and the Netherlands who did better technical work, furnished better text, and showed clearer and sharper impressions from types. His books tend toward excessive decoration and do not rival the finer books printed by Balthasar I Moretus. Nevertheless, he published on the grand scale, and his books reveal every peculiarity of typography that dazzled or astonished the publishing world of his day, just as Antwerp itself—and at the same time—dazzled the European Renaissance world.

Plantin's printing plant on the Vrijdagmarkt ("Friday Market") was a center of civilization in itself. Bold in his experimentation, especially before the Spanish Fury, he collected a select group of eminent draftsmen and engravers, including Pieter van der Borcht, Martin de Vos, and Jan and Hieronymus Wiericx.

In addition to having a close association with the scientists, humanists, and theologians who resided in or came to Antwerp, Plantin maintained a wide correspondence with intellectuals and important figures outside his adopted city. Indeed, the extant correspondence of Plantin shows that his printshop was a post office for the academic profession of Europe.

A brief listing of some of his important correspondents illustrates the extent to which the Plantin House was a center of civilization. Jehan le Clerc, scholar, and Martin de Jeune, printer-bookseller of Paris; François Fabricius, a classical scholar whose works were printed by Plantin; Stephanus Vinandus Phighius, Latin scholar and archeologist; Guillaume Symons, professor of theology at Louvain, who did some corrections for him; Corneille Valerius (Wouters), professor at Louvain; Herman Cruserius of Kampen, doctor of law and medicine and counselor of the duke of Cleves; Guillaume Roville, printer of Leon; Gabriel de Çayas, secretary to Philip II; Cardinal de Granvelle, trusted counselor of Philip II in the Netherlands, Italy, and Spain, and, along with Çayas, a constant and zealous patron of Plantin; King Philip II himself and the duke of Alva; Guillaume Lindanus, theologian and bishop, some of whose works Plantin printed; Jacques Pameleius (van Pamele), bishop of Saint Omer, one of the most learned theologians and men of letters of his time, for whom Plantin did some publishing; Augustin de Hasselt, a member of the Family of Love, whom Plantin helped establish in the printing business at Kampen; Guillaume Postel of France, one of the most learned men of his day, whose extreme religious opinions kept him on the run the greater part of his life and whose opinions approach those of Henry Niclaes of the Family; David Joris and Niclaes, the leading writers of the Family.

François Gerthols and Jacques Raevardus (Raewaerd), both of whom had works published by Plantin; Theodore Pulmannus (Poelman), the great Latin scholar about whom more will be said later; Jacques Cruguius, professor of Greek and Latin at Bruges, whose works on Horace were famous and for whom Plantin published; André Masius (Maes) (1515/16–1573), who knew Syrian, and for whom Plantin published three books; Alanus Cope, the English intellectual for whom Plantin published a work by Nicolas Harpsfield, who in turn spent the latter part of his life in the Tower by order of Elizabeth because he desired to remain loyal to the Catholic faith; Obertus Gifanius (von Giffen), legalist, philosopher, theologian, and professor at law in Germany and Bohemia, for whom Plantin did an annotated edition of Lucretius; Victor Giselenus, a medical student and corrector at Plantin's who published for him various classical works; George Buchanan, the Scottish theologian and poet who also published with Plantin, especially theological works; and Stanislas Hosius, the Polish cardinal who was a fighting foe of Lutheranism. The letters of these people in French, Latin, Dutch, Italian, and Spanish are an indication of the importance of Plantin to Europe's intellectual and theological life. They also provide an insight into the latitudinarian and cosmopolitan thought of the printer himself.

Many of the sixteen hundred editions Plantin printed were original works done at his request. His most productive year was 1575, when eighty-three editions were issued. The least productive was 1576, the year of the Spanish Fury, when only twenty-four editions appeared. His devotional books were more carefully printed and more richly illustrated than those of his rivals, and his school texts were much more carefully edited and more intelligently and scientifically arranged than those done by others. "All were of the first order; he did not pander to low appetites; his aims were always high and his tastes were severe."

He desired to be Europe's best printer—no more no less —and he was willing to work far beyond the efforts of the ordinary man to achieve this position. Of him Montanus said, "He is all spirit; he gives little thought to food or drink or repose. He loves to work." And work he did. Neither the Spanish Fury nor the siege of Antwerp nor the decline of the city's privileges and commerce nor the King's neglect nor his failure to perpetuate his name in a son nor the infirmities of old age shook his purpose. The Plantin-Moretus House outlasted the Spanish Hapsburgs, and his presses and types and printing shop, for which the city paid 1.2 million francs, are still the pride of Antwerp.

Although he far outdistanced his rivals, Plantin had many illustrious contemporaries in the sixteenth-century printing world of Antwerp. For example, his two deputies as "Arch-Typographer of the King," J. Werwithage and Amaat Tavernier, were well known to sixteenth-century book-dealers and printers.

Other typographers of sixteenth-century Antwerp who

followed the example of Plantin were Steelsius, and Graphaeus, already discussed, and van Diest. Also worthy of
mention is the ver Dussen family, Jan Trogesius and his
son Emanuel, and Martinus Nulius. In addition there were
the printers of music, such as Phalèse, about whom more
will be said later.

A printer of real distinction was Jan Beller, or Bellerus.
The beauty of his characters and the quality of his paper
made his books literary gems. His dictionaries were of real
value, especially his Latin-Spanish one. A good linguist
himself, he did translations from Italian, Portuguese, and
Spanish. Among his more popular and important books was
a book of manners, translated from the Tuscan, for young
ladies, and the *Vocabularius*, by Antonius Nebrissensius.

Also instrumental in propagating ideas were those sixteenth-century Antwerp printers who for one reason or
another—usually religious—left their native city to set up
presses elsewhere. Willem Sylvius, like Plantin and Raphelengius, was at one precarious time director of the Leiden
university press.

A large company of itinerant printers from Antwerp
took the printed word to foreign cities and countries.
Following paths pioneered by the traders, they were most
active in England, Germany, and the North Netherlands,
where they became, individually or collectively, influential
enough to be topics of special study in the printing history
of the areas to which they had fled. They were spokes
branching out from their cultural and radial hub on the
Scheldt.

In 1590, Balthazar Bellerus, son of Jan, set up a printshop
at Douai that continued in business into the eighteenth
century. Another son of Jan, the poet Luc, established one
of the oldest presses in Liège.

Gilles van den Rade, or Aegidius Radaeus, given citizenship in Antwerp June 1, 1571, was another who played a leading role in Antwerp printing before he emigrated. His table of proportional rates of monetary exchange for Antwerp as compared with other banking cities (797 pages)—brought forth in 1572 for a Lille citizen, François Flory—was an important contribution to international commerce. His other works have a wide and curious range of subject matter: proposed topics for competition by the Chambers of Rhetoric with refrain and musical notes; the remonstrance to the States-General by William of Orange, January 9, 1580; a book of Psalms by Philip van Marnix; a New Testament by Theodore Béza (1583); and job tasks for Plantin and other Antwerp printshops. Gilles II, established himself at Leeuwarden, and later in the province of Friesland. A second son, Jan, subsequently became printer to the province of Groningen.

An Antwerp name significant in Dutch printing is van Waesberghe, "who with the Elzevirs, also of Belgium origin, assuredly contributed to the typographic glory of Low Country printers in the seventeenth century." Jan I, who originally came from Aalst, was active in Antwerp during the mid-sixteenth century, and was enrolled in the Saint Lucas Guild there in May, 1557. Two years later he and several colleagues were put in the Steen, for printing and selling heretical books. He was freed April 20, 1570, and from his shop situated on the Kammenstraat, he busily plied his trade until 1585, when he moved to Rotterdam. By the middle of the sixteenth century, the van Waesberghe House, in book and atlas production, rivaled that of the more famous Elzevirs of Leiden and Amsterdam. The firm also published *Diversche liedekens* of Matthieu du Casteleyn, a book of love songs important in the development of Dutch poetry.

Other refugees often had more difficulty in putting down permanent roots because they tried and abused the patience and hospitality of their hosts, and were continually in confrontation with authority. These heroes, cranks, and sometimes martyrs to the cause of freedom of the press moved from place to place inventing new pseudonyms, altering their type fonts, and dodging inquisitors.

One of the most peripatetic and glamorous was Johannes van Hoochstraaten, often known by the pseudonym Hans Luft, of Marburg. He began his printing career in Antwerp in 1525, publishing for a time with Hadrianus Tilianus. Shortly, either at home or abroad, he was publishing books to advance the cause of Protestantism. The names of the authors for whom he printed in this phase of his life almost comprise a roster of Protestantism: Tyndale, Roy, Frith, and Bullinger, to mention a few. Hoochstraaten was in Antwerp until sometime between 1529 and 1531, publishing for the English market under various pseudonyms—Luft, Adam Anonymous, Basel, Peter Congeth, and Johannes Phidoponos.

He was active in Britain, Holland, Antwerp, Malmö, and Lübeck. At Malmö between 1535 and 1540 he published a series of Protestant books, mostly in Danish, under his own name, the Danish king, Christiern III, being favorable to the Reformation. Among his works in Scandinavia was an English translation of Christiern Pedersen's tract *The Richt vay to the Kingdon of Heuine.*

Stephen Mierdam also had close ties with Antwerp, England, and Germany. He was active in the former city in 1543, when he issued the first Spanish edition of the New Testament, translated by Francisco der Enzinas. This book is beautifully done in Roman letter with excellent woodcut illustrations.

The two van Ruremond brothers, Hans and Christopher, were courageous Antwerp printers. Christopher was one of the first to issue Reformation books for the English market, among them two Sarum Services Books and a Tyndale New Testament, for which he was arraigned through the efforts of the English diplomatic agent in Antwerp. Ruremond defended himself by insisting that English laws could not apply in the domains of the emperor Charles V, albeit a goodly number of the New Testaments were destined for British readers.

Ruremond won his case, but it was tantamount to winning an opening round. On January 16, 1527, an imperial edict forbade not only the printing of the New Testaments but also the possession of them. They were subsequently all burned, and so thorough were the authorities that there is no extant copy of the 1526 Tyndale by van Ruremond. Christopher went to England about 1530 or 1531, where he was either executed or died in prison. Fox recorded in the *Book of Martyrs* under the year 1531: "An Antwerp Bookseller named Christopher for selling New Testaments *In English to John Row, Bookbinder, was thrown into prison at Westminster* and then died."

Hans had an even stormier career. In 1525 he, along with Christopher, had printed a Dutch Bible, and as a result, on October 30 of that year, he was charged before the town council of Antwerp with printing a heretical Lutheran book, and banished. He was arrested in London. Listed among those who in 1528 were forced to abjure their faith was "Jan Raimund, a Dutchman; for causing 1500 of Tyndale's New Testaments to be printed at Antwerp and for bringing 500 into England."

After his brother's death, Hans left England for Antwerp but was soon back in London. He edited an edition of the New Testament in 1538 and translated the *Exposition on the Song of the Blessed Virgin Mary*.

The list could be expanded almost indefinitely: Adriaen van Berghen, whose *Arnold's Chronicle* contained the earliest text of *The Nutbrown Maid*; Emmanuel Meteren, historian as well as printer; Jan van Doesborch, whose accounts of "recent discoveries" may have influenced Richard Hakluyt; Pieter Craesbeeck, who established a famous press at Lisbon; François Billet, who established another at Saint Omer; and others less significant.

Notable Antwerp booksellers in England were Peter Kaetz, agent for Christopher van Ruremond; Francis Byrckmans, whom Erasmus said was "wont to import nearly all books into England"; John Birchman, agent of Plantin; John Boeidens, outlet for Thierry Martins; Joyce Pelgrim, who was connected with the book trade in both Oxford and London; John Gubkyn, associated with Mierdam; and Nicholas Spierinck, university stationer, located in King's Parade, Cambridge.

These are only a few of the best-known bookmen. Many others were either not so successful or did not find their way into the chronicles or records. The known and the unknown, however, made the dissemination of knowledge easier, and it was from their presses and shops that the heady, intoxicating ideas of the northern Renaissance and Reformation took wing. Some were noble characters; some were not. Some labored like serfs, threatened at times by both poverty and government; others lived luxuriously and were respected members of the community. Whatever the standard, however—whether economic success or contribution to the world of scholarship and learning—no other bookman measured up to Plantin, around whose printing house the intellectual, and much of the artistic, activity of Europe during the late sixteenth and early seventeenth centuries revolved.

CHAPTER V

"A smackering of . . . Grammar"

A successful printing and publishing trade requires a reading public, and Plantin could be sure that Antwerp would absorb a substantial number of his works. But what sort of a populace was it that could consume the multilingual texts pouring from the Antwerp presses? A populace with such an insatiable thirst that many publishing projects ran into multiple editions. One fortunate author was Guicciardini, who commented: "They all haue some smackering of their Grammar, and euery one, yea euery husbandman can write and read."

He went further in his praise of literate Antwerp to claim that some people knew as many as six or seven languages, and it was common for citizens of both sexes to be able to handle three or four adequately. French, second only to Flemish, was the most used language, followed in order by Spanish and Latin. Guicciardini himself took language lessons at the school of Josse Verrebroeck (Velaraeus), which specialized in Greek and Hebrew.

In spite of Anglo-Antwerp trade, English was less commonly spoken in the city than it is today. Scholars like Sir Thomas More could easily move about in Antwerp without it, because Latin was their "Esperanto." Also, England in this period was not one of the cultural wells from which Antwerp drew. In 1534 there appeared in the city a *Dictionarus quinque linguarum*, which included Dutch,

French, Spanish, Latin, and Italian. In 1540 a new edition entitled *Dictionarus septem linguarum* added English and German. Jan I Moretus could speak seven languages, but not English.

Antwerp admittedly had its intellectuals, but how far did the learning reach down into the lower classes? On the primary level, that of the "three R's," education seems to have been widespread. The artisans, burghers, and shopkeepers then as now needed a basic education to conduct their activities. Some schooling was offered by charitable foundations, but more by ecclesiastical or private institutions. The poetess Anna Bijns (1494–1575), grew up close to a well-known school, De Patience on the Keiserstraat, which her brother Martin attended. Anna probably learned secondhand from her brother, whose education was a severe financial drain on the fatherless Bijns family. Whether she learned from Martin, nuns, or some other source, Anna—a spinster throughout her life—received sufficient training to become the foremost poet in the Netherlands of her day. Furthermore, her command of Scripture and the classics was fairly competent.

Anna in 1536 was entered in the Saint Ambrose Guild, the guild for teachers. She rented from Jan van Severdonck, the chaplain of Saint Mary's, Het Roosterken, a house across the street from her brother, where she lived, wrote, and taught school until 1573.

Alexander Graphaeus ("De Schryver") received much of his education from Cornelis, his more famous father, who operated a private school on an advanced level before he became secretary of the city. Schools similar to those attended by Martin Bijns and Graphaeus must have been numerous. Although the Latin School attached to Our Lady's Church was in 1521 the only authorized one, additional ones were later set up in each of Antwerp's four parishes. And there were others. A cathedral song school was established when Antwerp became a bishopric, and many teachers of elementary schools must have included some Latin in their offerings because of its universality. Pieter Heyns, at one time dean of Saint Ambrose's Guild, bought a house in the rue des Augustines, which became a celebrated school, emphasizing geography, French, and Flemish.

Since it had no major university and was neither a center of government nor an ecclesiastical center until the second half of the century, Antwerp had an educational system geared primarily to the needs of industry and commerce. This is not to say that all learning was vocational. The University of Louvain was not far away, and gifted students could matriculate there or in other European universities. Generally, however, Antwerp's young men did not continue their education far beyond the age of fifteen. If the family were wealthy or had foreign connections, formal instruction might be rounded out by travel.

In addition to languages, utilitarian Antwerp educators stressed arithmetic, geometry, and general science. Consequently, many intellectuals practiced architecture, and a goodly number of stonecutters and carpenters showed a knowledge of mechanics and geometry admirable even today. Furthermore, many powerful merchants, as youngsters, had been instilled with an interest in learning and in the classics. Some became amateur scholars; others patronized scholarly undertakings either by direct subsidy or by purchasing for their own libraries the products of the Antwerp presses. Most of the leading scholar-merchant-statesmen were bibliophiles, or at least collectors. Plantin built his library primarily for reference, whereas the geographer Abraham Ortelius was a scientist, antiquarian, and collector. For the less affluent, Antwerp had a city library used by Erasmus, for one, who did some private tutoring in Antwerp.

Women were educated privately, by religious foundations, or at girls' schools such as the Lauwerboom ("Laurel Tree"), which was operated by the Heyns family. Catherine Plantin—admittedly not run-of-the-mill either intellectually or in background—at age thirteen read proof in five languages on the Polyglot Bible with Arias Montanus. There are innumerable examples of widows who took over their husbands' businesses, some of these in the printing and book trade. The mother of Janus Gruter, in addition to being able to read Galen in the original, knew four other languages.

The Lauwerboom between 1576 and 1585 enrolled 464 girls who came from some of the best Netherlands families in most of the seventeen provinces. About half of Heyns's students, about fifteen young ladies at a time, boarded at his house. They learned how to run a home, entertain, and prepare for a role in society suitable to their station. Day students paid about ten florins a year, and boarders ten times that amount. All students participated in the various school activities, which ranged from devotions to language drills, from needlework to acting in dramas written by the master and others.

The Plantin correspondence provides a delightful example of a day in the life of an Antwerp schoolboy. Plantin's fourteen-year-old grandson Christophe, who his grandfather said "cares for nothing but books," crossed the old patriarch. For punishment he was compelled to write in Latin a description of his day:

"The occupations of Christophe Beys, February 21,

1587. I got up at half-past 6 o'clock. I went to embrace my grandfather and grandmother. Then I took breakfast. Before 7 o'clock I went to my class and well recited my lesson in syntax. At 8 o'clock I heard mass. At half-past 8 I had learned my lesson in Cicero and I had fairly recited it. At 11 o'clock I returned to the house and studied my lesson in phraseology. After dinner I went back to the class and properly recited my lesson. At half-past 2 I had fairly recited my lesson in Cicero. At 4 o'clock I went to hear a sermon. Before 6 o'clock I returned to the house, and I read proof on *Libellus Sodalitatis* with my cousin Francis (Raphelengius). I showed myself refractory while reading the proofs of the book. Before supper, my grandfather having made me go to him, to repeat what I had heard preached, I did not wish to go nor to repeat; and even when others desired me to ask pardon of grandfather, I was unwilling to answer. Finally I have showed myself in the eyes of all, proud, stubborn and willful. After supper I have written my occupations for this day, and I have read them to grandfather. The end crowns the work."

A school of note was the Papenschool at Our Lady's run by the humanist Rumoldus Verdonck (1541–1620). It was situated on Milk Street just behind the Cathedral. It was highly successful and numbered among its pupils Peter Paul Rubens and Balthasar Moretus.

The educational institutions created a demand for texts which the printers were happy to meet. A book of letters of the alphabet with rhymed couplets and woodcut illustrations was an early forerunner of the ABC books of Old and New England. The *Colloquies* and *Adages* of Erasmus were popular, and Pieter Heyns translated the former into French and Netherlands. Josse Verrebroeck did numerous volumes from the Greek into Latin. To help his students study Greek, he translated thirty-seven dialogues from the *Paedologia* of Petrus Mossallanus into that language. Perhaps the title "Dean of Antwerp humanists of the late sixteenth century" is too exaggerated an accolade for Verrebroeck, but surely one cannot quibble with his student Guicciardini who considered him "Dean of teachers of the humanities."

Heyns's educational books ranged from an ABC book printed by Plantin in 1568 to an *Insroction de la lecture françois* and *Du fondement de l'arithmetique* which Plantin brought out in 1584. Instruction books in French and Flemish, books on the drama with some bad plays written by himself, included *A Mirror of Magistrates, A Mirror of the World*, dictionaries, writing books, psalm books, deportment books, and guides for religious instruction turned out for his "Nymphs of the Laurel Tree." In addition, he adopted for them such texts as *Lettres missives familieres*, by Gerard de Vevre. One of Heyns's best texts for language instruction placed emphasis on both the spoken and the written word. The work was printed by Plantin in 1571 and entitled *Cort ondervvys van de acht delen der Francoischer talen tot voorderinge en profijt der Duytscher ioncheryt* ("Short Instruction in Eight Parts of the French Language for the Improvement and Profit of Dutch Young Ladies").

Scriptures were taught in most schools in one form or another. There were various guides for young students, the most famous being the *Beginsel van wijsheid* ("Beginning of Wisdom"). Two of the best editions were printed in Antwerp, the first in 1552 by Jan van Ghelen and a later one in 1564 by Jan van Waesberghe. This last work steels the young to face joy and adversity, and it reeks with philosophizing. The most popular book for the young in the sixteenth and seventeenth centuries was *Den utersten wille* ("The Utmost Desire") of Lowys Porguin, which was printed for the first time by Amaat Tavernier of Antwerp.

Three books by Nicholas Brontius, brought out by Simon Cock in Antwerp between 1540 and 1541, give instruction in Latin, Greek, and Hebrew, each chapter dealing with one of the seven liberal arts. Twenty woodcuts illustrate how Renaissance teachers in northern Europe tended to combine the Scriptures and the classics.

Language was the queen of subjects, and men of letters were concerned mainly with philology. In the sixteenth century, Netherlands (modern Dutch) was emerging from the Middle Ages and making giant strides toward becoming a language of science and letters. Having held its own against medieval Latin, it was now threatened by classicism. The vernacular had its Dutch defenders, although none of them was a du Bellay. Jan van de Werve, a well-born citizen of Antwerp, wrote in 1553 the *Trescor der Diutsche tale* ("Treasury of the Dutch Language"), a plea against imitating other languages, especially the Romance ones: "Help me, I ask you to raise up our mother language which now lies concealed in the earth like gold, so we may prove how needless it is for us to beg the assistance of other languages."

Heyns labored to clean up Flemish, but not without considerable purism and pedantry. He did succeed, however, in eradicating a number of foreign words which were creeping into the language. His school for girls stressed education in French and Dutch, and his *Den Nederlandtschen landtspieghel* ("The Netherlands Mirror of the World") did much to popularize the vernacular. Simon Steven, one-time Antwerp accountant, who also wrote on science and optics, in *De beghinseln der weegconst* ("An Introduction to the Art of Weights"), which appeared in 1548, pled for the use of the mother tongue in scientific works. Johannes Goropius, that jack-of-all-trades and friend of Montanus, claimed in the *Origines Antverpianae* (Plantin, 1569) that his studies in Latin, Greek, Hebrew, and Old German had convinced him that Flemish, the language of the Franks, was the oldest language in the world and the mother of all other tongues, the classicists Joseph Scaliger and Lipsius to the contrary notwithstanding.

Another pioneer in the Flemish revival was Cornelis Kiel, one of Plantin's best editors and proofreaders. Half-blind from his labors, Kiel published at Plantin's in 1573 a *Dictionarium Teutonic-Latinum*. Part of the *Thesarus Teutonicae linguae*, Kiel's Flemish-Latin dictionary, did much to reinvigorate Flemish and to "standardize its still uncertain spelling." He also translated into Netherlands a Latin grammar by Brechtanus, a portion of Philippe de Commines' history, and the *Description of the Low Countries* by Guicciardini, which was printed in 1612 at Amsterdam, five years after the translator's death. The Flemish dictionary, of which Plantin was "ungenerously envious," was, however, Kiel's most lasting contribution to philology and the Dutch language.

Notwithstanding the efforts of Goropius, Heyns, and Kiel, it was the Chambers of Rhetoric, those "sole guardians of Dutch poetry," says Professor Geyl, that preserved and enriched the Flemish vernacular during the Middle Ages and played a significant, though florid, role in harmonizing it with the medieval, the Renaissance, and the modern. Members of the leading Antwerp chamber, joined the Brabant chamber in Amsterdam, but Renaissance individualism did not free itself from convention until the North Holland chamber in Amsterdam became dominant.

The origins of the chambers are obscure. One theory is that they were the result of the long tradition of court music dating back at least to Charlemagne and revived by the trouvères. Another theory is that they were an outgrowth of the Crusades. At first they were highly religious, and they flourished in the Low Countries under Burgundian rule. Their performances and displays were quite popular in Antwerp during the fifteenth and sixteenth centuries. Antwerp's first chamber, "the Violet," was founded in 1480 by certain members of the Saint Lucas Guild. Ten years later a second chamber, "the Marigold," was operating, and in that year the magistrates gave both groups handsome subsidies for their services. A third chamber, "the Olive Branch," was founded about 1510.

The chambers had a governing body on which the prince and the captain were the two leading officials. Actually the "facteur" held the most important post, since he assigned roles, organized the performances, and directed the poetical exercises of the younger members. He composed verses for special occasions, and—with the *Kerkmeesters*—worked with the guilds in planning religious ceremonies. The chambers, very social, provided members with funds for banquets, festive celebrations, and masses for the souls of the departed. In winter, Sundays were reserved for poetic recitations or dramatic performances. These were usually written by the members, and attendance at the meetings was closely restricted.

On great occasions such as the Joyous Entry of a ruler, the chambers devised histories or plays and performed them on the public square. When in 1495 the Saint Lucas Guild received papal permission to establish the Brotherhood of the Seven Sorrows of Our Lady at Our Lady's Church, the Violet—composed primarily of Guild members —honored the event by presenting a play of twenty-eight hundred verses.

With the public, gatherings called *Landjewels* ("Land Jubilees") were the most popular. These were held from time to time by the chief towns, who invited all the chambers in the various towns to participate. Prizes were given for size of the delegation, elaborateness of livery of the performers, and performances. Winning depended on the skill of the artists, the overall financial contributions of the Town Fathers, and the ingenuity of the "facteur."

The highlight of the festival was a question put to the competitors. This question was always religious, such as, "What is the greatest favor God has accorded for the salvation of mankind?" The first *Landjewel* was held in Antwerp in 1495. Henceforth all the Antwerp chambers appeared in most of the competitions, but the Violet won most of the prizes.

The Burgundian dukes, and later the Hapsburgs and the Church, had misgivings about the *Landjewels*. Often democratic or heretical statements made there inflamed the crowds against the existing order. The chambers' reception of Charles V in 1520, which included performances by half-naked women, must have caused the Church considerable uneasiness; but that occasion did not approach in effrontery the *Landjewel* held at Ghent in 1539, where many answers put to the question were highly offensive to the clergy. By that time the Violet was already a hotbed of heresy. The Ghent question had been, "What would be the greatest consolation to one on the point of death?" The Violet's prize-winning answer was "The Resurrection of the Flesh." Three years before the Ghent affair, the Dominicans had prodded the magistrates to forbid the chambers to perform any more comedies without authorization by the order and the town officials.

Time would soon strike the blithe spirit of the chambers with the sword of discontent. In May, 1547, Peter Schuddemate, a schoolmaster and member of the Violet was beheaded at Antwerp for writing heretical *spelen van sinne* ("serious plays"). Permission to hold the *Landjewel* at Antwerp in 1561 was given only under duress. This was perhaps the greatest gathering of all, with 1,393 mounted Rhetoricians accompanied by 23 show wagons and 197 smaller ones. The "facteur" of the Violet would subsequently be branded a heretic, but for the moment the pageantry and the great stage built by the artist Cornelis de Vriendt camouflaged the impending trouble. Soon the chambers would be staging hollow entrances for one politician after another as successive tides of Protestant and Catholic hate engulfed the city. The 1561 spectacle cost Antwerp one hundred thousand florins. The organizer, Antoine van Straelen, was one of the most popular men in the city. That popularity and the opinions expressed by the Rhetoricians placed his neck under the executioner's axe in 1567.

Professor Geyl claimed, "The poetry of the Rhetoricians was an off shoot of the medieval spirit, whose . . . inspiration . . . was exhausted." He condemned such ingenious tricks as double rhymes, chain rhymes, and pretentious words, which are found in their writings. Yet they strove for innovation in their verse. Humanism was in evidence, but, as Geyl says, "A really high standard could not possibly be maintained in the circle of those excellent and merry citizens. Only some of the verses of Anna Bijns . . . are still alive with the passion [with] which she defended the

Catholic Church against the schismatics of her day." The vogue called for Latin poetry, and writing in the vernacular was often left to the less learned.

Like the genre painters, the Rhetoricians produced much that was bad. On the other hand, they contributed to the development of various poetic forms and uses of language, and their popularity led to an increased taste for dramatic verse. It is unfair to dismiss the bulk of Antwerp's sixteenth-century literature as wholly unimaginative, meaningless, and pompous. It was not that bad. The plays produced by the chamber were dramatic historical accounts based mostly on the Bible—didactic plays, morality plays, and dramas dealing with the lives of saints. Farces *(klucht-spelen)* and morality plays *(zinnespelen)* might be the usual fare dished out at the *Landjewel* gatherings, but at chamber meetings there was greater variety. Those offerings—crude, wordy, bawdy, fervent, religious, and sweet—were nevertheless forerunners of Bredero's comedies and Vondel's tragedies.

Everyman, originally a Flemish play, was probably first translated into English at Antwerp. In 1500, Roland van den Dorp printed this along with a number of dramas, as did Willem Vosterman. Peter Schuddemate's play against the placards of Charles V cost him his head. The poet Jean Baptiste Houwaert (1533–99) wrote a terrible rhymed indictment of Alva's atrocities, *De vier uiterste van de dod* ("The Four Extremes of Death"), which was printed by Plantin in 1558. Houwaert also wrote an allegory denouncing Rome, entitled *Milenus clachte, waer in de groote tirannye der Romeynen verhaelt* ("The Complaint of Milenus on the Great Tyranny of Rome"). Guillaume van Haecht, a "facteur" of the Violet, wrote three morality plays based on the Apostles, and a miracle play on the conversion of Saint Paul. His morality plays were soon on the Index, and he was forced to flee Antwerp. Jan Baptist van der Noot, who was born near Antwerp in 1539 and probably died there, wrote a long work in which he showed his Calvinist commitment with dire predictions about the fate of worldlings. Entitled *The Theater for Worldlings*, the allegorical work with its famous woodcuts had many English editions and translations, one of the latter being done by the poet Edmund Spenser. The earliest known performance of a classical play in Dutch took place in Antwerp in 1494. Thereafter, Dutch plays with classical themes, a number of which van Houwaert wrote, became fairly common in Antwerp.

Such authors did not live in the medieval world of fantasy, but were harbingers of the new age. Their chamber and *Landjewel* performances made the theater an active force—so active that chamber and dramatist often felt the lash of authority. These writers also carried their causes beyond the theater. Haecht did three laments over the treatment of his coreligionists, the Lutherans, and in 1597 published a volume of psalms and canticles to be used by Lutherans in Antwerp and Brussels. Later, in exile, he composed a number of patriotic verses, the most famous being the *Guesen liedtboek* ("Beggars' Songbook"), the songbook of the revolt. Van Houwaert did religious poems, along with a good deal of occasional verse, as did Frans Fraet of the Violet, whose *t'Palays der gheleerde ingienen* ("The Palace of Scholarly Devices") had over a hundred moral figures.

Jacob de Mol, Peter Cassiere, and Pieter Heyns also composed religious poetry, as did Lambert Goetman, a forerunner of Jacob Cats, but the two most outstanding figures in this area were Cornelis Crul and Anna Bijns. Crul also wrote plays and a delightful ABC book. His best poem is *Mondt toe borse toe gracie*, and the most famous is *Heynken de luyere*. Since Erasmus was his guide and example in matters of religion, he was more moderate in his views than the fighting Anna, but both saw the new heresies like the old ones as a threat to Christ's Church and Christ's kingdom on earth.

Without doubt, Crul was Antwerp's best Rhetorical poet. He has a freshness in his verse which foreshadows Bredero, both in his farces and in his love of the pastoral. One genre poem of thanksgiving starts as follows:

> *You who make little apples, pears, and nuts*
> *Be praised for your good cheer,*
> *For meat and fish which taste so good,*
> *For bread, for butter, for wine, for beer.*

The verse suffers in my translation.

Anna Bijns was the poet laureate of Catholic Antwerp and the best lyricist of her day. Perhaps secretly, but platonically, loving a Minorite, Anna attacked the new creeds with all the vehemence at her command. To her, Luther was the devil's instrument, and everything from famine to war was blamed on his pernicious doctrines. She appeared on the literary scene about 1520, and eight years later Jacob van Liesveldt published her first volume of poems under the title *Refereinen . . . meer suers dan soets* ("Refrains More Sour Than Sweet"). The twenty-three poems in the work were all sharp satires on the Reformation, and they caused a considerable stir in and out of Antwerp. A second bundle of *Refereinen*, twenty-four new poems, appeared in 1548, and the next to the last poem was made into a Latin song by the Minorite and humanist Brechtanus.

In spite of the acidity and intricate rhyme schemes, her

language has purity. She loved to balance one part of a line against the rest of it. For example:

> *Is God met mij, wie sal mij schaden*
> *("If God is with me, who can harm me?")*

Some of the love songs were written with charm and tenderness. They complain of unrequited love and faithless lovers, and their passionate tone indicates that they are perhaps autobiographical.

Lucas de Heere published the first sonnet in Netherlands in 1565, *Den hof en boomgaerd der peosien* ("The Garden and Orchard of Poetry"). Admittedly he was influenced by Marot and Ronsard. Yet as Professor Leonard Forster points out, he first learned the sonnet form in Antwerp, perhaps from Frans Floris under whom he studied painting and who at the time was well known for his poetic powers. Matthieu du Casteleyn wrote a number of love poems with a fine lyric quality which contributed to the development of Dutch poetry. His poems were designed to be set to music, and, although loaded with clichés, they are highly lyrical. For example:

> *Her speech affects me joyously*
> *She speaks the words of poetry.*

Another lyric poet of significance was Jan van der Noot, whose lyrics were superior to those of most of his contemporaries. His ambition was to do for Dutch literature what Ronsard had done for French writing. Earlier he had been influenced by Marot and Petrarch. Several of his sonnets place him among the good poets of the sixteenth century. His two outstanding literary achievements, *Het bosken* ("The Thicket," about 1570) and *Het boek van extase* ("The Book of Ecstasy," 1575) reflect the chamber. The latter book, often entitled the *Olympiads*, first appeared in a German edition. Some years later van der Noot brought out the first half of it in a French-Dutch edition. This has been called the first great modern narrative of the Dutch Renaissance, and it combines "medieval worship of women" and allegory with "an absolutely modern tone and atmosphere." It is not a run-of-the-mill imitation of the French or Italian. The meter is van der Noot's own, as are the phrases and metaphors. It is allegory par excellence. In the *Lofsang van Braband* ("Songs in Praise of Brabant," 1580), the "Patriot of Antwerp" heaped praise on his native province, to which he returned from exile, much to the chagrin of the ardent Protestants.

The songs of the Beggars, mostly anonymous, form another collection of Dutch literature having verve and spirit. "Now hopeful, then despondent, stately and vehement, expressing scorn or hatred, sorrow or confidence, these songs preserve the memory of an arresting period of Netherlands history with a freshness unequaled by chronicles of documents." Although the victorious north Calvinists appropriated the treasure of the *Guesen liedtboek* as their own, many of the best songs were written by Antwerpians and Brabanters. Among them was Guillaume van Haecht. The governor of Antwerp during the last days of its freedom, the Brabanter Marnix de St. Aldegonde was probably the author of the *Wilhelmus*, the greatest of the Beggar songs and today the Dutch national anthem.

Marnix in addition translated psalms and wrote sonnets. He also did a prose work, *The Beehive of the Holy Roman Church* (1570), a scathing attack on Catholicism. For the first time Dutch prose was used in a pamphlet by a man equally at home in French and Latin.

Other types of Dutch prose were very much in vogue.

The oldest printed version of the *Story of Roland* came from the shop of W. Vorsterman early in the sixteenth century. In 1516 he published a romantic story of Margriete of Lymborch. Soon the market was flooded with other romances. Popular themes in addition to Margriete were stories about Jan Uit den Veigiere, Merlin, and Urbaen, the unrecognized son of Frederick Barbarossa. Also in demand were translations from Boccacio and French writers of romances. Two popular Dutch romances were *Mariken van Nieumeghen* and the *Historie van Thijh Ulenspiegel*.

Histories and chronicles also sold. In 1497, Roland van den Dorp printed the *Aldersexcellentste cronike van Brabant*. In 1512 (perhaps) and in 1518 and 1530, Jan van Doesborch printed chronicles of the same province. W. Vorsterman in 1531 printed *De excellente cronicke van Vlanderen*, by Andries Smet of Bruges. Mention has already been made of the *Origines Antverpianae* of Johannes Goropius. Furthermore, no study of sixteenth-century Antwerp and the Low Countries can be written without consulting Emmanuel van Meteren's monumental and multivolume history of the religious conflict.

Modern journalism was born in Antwerp. The city was a tremendous depository for news. Moreover, the traders were insatiable in their demand for news coverage, because political happenings influenced the market. The Fuggers distributed news sheets entitled *d'Ordinare zeitung* at all of their outlets if the news affected house business. These and other flyers appeared intermittently. About 1605, just beyond the scope of this study, Abraham Verhoeven of Antwerp conceived the idea of creating a periodic news-pamphlet which would regularly cover European events. It first appeared May 7, 1605, under the title *Nieuwe tydinghen*. It had woodcut illustrations and carried news of a battle currently being waged outside Antwerp's city walls. It concluded with the old Antwerp expression "of het waer is, zal den tijd leeren" ("if it is true, then time shall teach it"). Thus the periodic newspaper came into being.

CHAPTER VI

"To gaze in these books"

I N spite of champions of use of the vernacular, Latin remained the language of the intellectual world. Although
Latin provided a vehicle whereby learning could transcend
linguistic boundaries, in the Netherlands its use erected a
partition between scholars and the masses.

Antwerp, however, had such a broad educational base
that communication between intellectual and ordinary citizen was easier than it was elsewhere. Many amateurs made
significant contributions to scholarship, and others, such
as printers, were in part dependent for their livelihoods on
the fruits of scholarship. A goodly number of burghers had
sampled the classics in school, and a taste for them remained
after they had entered the world of business and government. To the question posed in 1581 by the geographer
Georg Braun—"What could be more pleasant than in one's
own home free from all dangers, to gaze in these books . . .
looking at the pictures and reading the texts accompanying
them, to acquire knowledge . . . ?"—they would have an-
swered, "Nothing!"

Peter Gilles, or Aegidius, who knew both Latin and
Greek, is an excellent example of the amateur scholar whose
outside interests placed him in the middle of the intellectual
currents of his time. He was born in Antwerp in 1486, and
died there in 1533. He lived a tranquil life, dividing his

time between holding office as *greffier* ("treasurer") and reading and producing literary works.

Like Plantin he had a wide circle of friends and corresponded with "in a word all the remarkable men of this period." Sir Thomas More was his houseguest and the godfather of one of his children. Albrecht Dürer dined at his table, and another famous artist, Quentin Massys, did his portrait and that of Erasmus as a gift for More. The accompanying verse compared the two to Castor and Pollux. Need more be said? Erasmus considered him "a man of great knowledge and at the same time of great modesty, having a bonhomie about him that could be firm without being malicious."

The story of Massys's companion portraits provides a delightful insight into Aegidius' relationship with the two northern humanists. Aegidius knew Erasmus prior to 1514 when Erasmus asked him to care for "one square wooden box tied with cord and three French trunks covered with leather." He met More a year later, and as a result More had his meeting with the Portuguese mariner Raphael Hythloday in front of Our Lady's Church. At the time Aegidius was talking to Amerigo Vespucci's former crewman. The three then went to More's lodgings and sat and talked, and Hythloday told his tale of Utopia. Erasmus was visiting Aegidius when More sent the manuscript of *Utopia* to the Antwerp statesman.

The two in 1517 decided to send More a present. They commissioned Massys to paint their portraits so that they could be framed together. The work was delayed first because Aegidius became ill, and secondly because, as Erasmus says: "Somehow or other it occurred to my doctor to order some pills for the purging of bile, and what he was fool enough to prescribe, I was idiot enough to take. The portrait was already begun, but when I returned to the painter after taking the physic, he said it was not the same face; so the painting has been put off for some days till I can look more cheerful."

In spite of pest and pill, the painting which More had been "greedily" awaiting was finished by autumn. Aegidius was depicted holding a letter addressed to him in More's handwriting, and Erasmus was busily engaged in paraphrasing the Epistle to the Romans.

More was delighted with the gift. Although religious controversy was to fracture Europe, and the portraits were to be separated, the friendship of the three held fast. The *Utopia* was dedicated to Aegidius, who had it published at Louvain the year of the portraits. For Erasmus, Aegidius first edited the *Letters of Illustrious Men*, then a collection of Aesop's *Fables* translated into Latin, and finally, with Cornelis Graphaeus, the *Enchiridion*.

A legalist by profession, Aegidius wrote a number of short scientific law treatises. He also compiled an abridgment of Roman law designed primarily for students. His most popular work was an abridgment of Roman law drawn up by the Visigoths. His writings were a vital contribution to Renaissance legal studies, and were complemented in 1567 by Plantin's ten-volume edition of the *Corpus juris civilis*.

For his publisher, Thierry Martins, Aegidius edited the works of Plato, Isocrates, Angelo Poliziano, Rudolphus Agricola, and others. These editions are clean, clear-cut, and well done, and they filled a need at the time for legal and classical texts. In an epithalamium, Erasmus has the Muses say: "We believe you must needs know that most courteous and accomplished youth in all Kinds of Polite Learning, Petrus Aegidius."

Cornelis Graphaeus (1482–1558) and his son Alexander (1519 to *c.* 1575) also combined a government position with scholarship. Because of their writings and the fact that each was subsequently secretary to the town magistrates, they carried the name "Scribonus" or "De Schryver" ("writer"), and are often listed under the surname "Schryver." The father was a schoolteacher, government official, poet, artist, and musician. He knew Latin and Greek, had traveled to Italy, and was one of the first in Antwerp to adopt Lutheranism. He was also one of Luther's first apostates, but for a time his religion cost him his post as secretary.

In and out of office, he pursued a literary life. He translated and wrote poetical verse—some of a political nature, and some in which he described his native city with all its wonders. He wrote two excellent language textbooks, and enjoyed an exaggerated reputation for both oratory and poetry.

The great name in Netherlands scholarship after Erasmus was Justus Lipsius (1547–1606), who was born between Brussels and Louvain. After a long and brilliant career in many lands and at many academic institutions, he returned to Louvain and died there, mourned by much of the scholarly world, Catholic and Protestant alike. Plantin published the greater part of his works and paid him well— a departure from his treatment of other scholars. Furthermore, there was a room at Plantin's home-printshop set aside solely for use by the famous humanist. Lipsius taught at Catholic Louvain, Lutheran Jena, and Calvinist Leiden. He followed the forms of worship observed by the university to which he was at the time attached, but he ended up a Catholic.

Although he was involved in a number of theological

controversies, including one with Dirck Coornhert over toleration, the majority of his works were historical rather than metaphysical. Seventeenth-century Cambridge might become excited over Tacitus, but in Lipsius's time the great issues were such imponderables as grace, predestination, and justification by faith. His writings varied from studies in early German history and early law to histories dealing with the growth of the cult of the Virgin at Halle or the cult of the Hebrews. His *Politiques* was placed on the Index. No man was ever more honored in his lifetime. Princes, sages, and Antwerp burghers paid homage to him. On his death, a collection of obituary verses printed at Antwerp were written by authors both Catholic and Protestant, and the town fathers purchased a stone memorial for his grave.

Francis Raphelengius (1539–97) like Lipsius had close associations with Antwerp and Leiden. Born at Lannoy, he was educated at Ghent, Nürnberg, Paris, and Cambridge. When he was about twenty, he went to Antwerp. He had joined Plantin's firm by 1564, and the next year married the boss's daughter. Two years after his marriage, he was enrolled in Saint Lucas Guild as a master printer. He purchased a bookshop close to Our Lady's and spent the period up to 1585 correcting texts for his father-in-law, selling books, living on a handsome dowry, and editing five books, all but one of which were published by Plantin.

The range of his titles is interesting because it provides some indication of the reading tastes of the Antwerpians. He edited a translation by Cornelis Kiel of a history of Louis XI and Charles the Bold of Burgundy by Philippe de Commines, a companion set of two volumes by Jean Marconville on the good and bad points to be found in women, and the complaints of Bartholomew de las Casas about Spanish cruelties to the natives in the New World. He also edited the letters of Cardinal Granvelle and seven penitential psalms. Of his erudition, Arias Montanus said, "No one surpassed him in his knowledge of ancient languages."

At Leiden, where Raphelengius became university printer in 1589, he embraced Calvinism. Soon he became professor of Hebrew. While on the faculty, he compiled a book of Arabic characters, followed eventually by an Arabic dictionary. In this endeavor, he received much encouragement from his old Antwerp friends, Ortelius the geographer, and Clusius and Dodoens the botanists. Thus Arabic studies, for which Leiden subsequently became so well known, received initial impetus from an Antwerp refugee.

Raphelengius's son Jean, who remained a Catholic, was consequently barred from the post of university printer. Between 1613 and 1622 he sold back to the Plantin-Moretus printers the fonts, matrixes, and woodcuts that had been willed to his father. Thus did the famous herbal and emblem plates return home to Antwerp. Jean, like his father, cultivated Latin poetry along with philology.

Somewhat less well known was Théodore Poelman, a fuller by day and an editor at night. He was badly exploited by Plantin, who used his texts and eventually fell heir to his excellent manuscript library. Poelman customarily worked with established Latin authors and purified their texts, a task that did much to advance scholarship both in his own and in subsequent generations.

Although Plantin himself was partial to the classics and the humanities, he was not blind to other branches of learning. His close association with Ortelius, Dodoens, Clusius, and Guicciardini add luster to his accomplishments, and he was not alone in his interest in botany and cartography. The city was a mecca for mariners who moved along the quays discussing lands, flora, and fauna newly discovered. At the Exchange there was a real interest in the emerging sciences, if only for commercial reasons. The practical Antwerpians nurtured engineers, agriculturalists, botanists, and cartographers far more than did the Italians. From Antwerp the new ideas and new learning radiated to those parts of Europe whither went the ships and wagons.

The scientific writers avoided much of the dilettantism, bad taste, and pedantry that marred studies in the humanities. They were more direct and to the point, much more individualistic, and less dependent on the Ancients. Andrew Vesalius at Brussels linked anatomy with medicine, as the botanists tied botany with pharmacology, and as Simon Steven and his ilk joined mathematics and physics to surveying and engineering.

The intelligent classification and conscientious description of plants by Dodoens, Clusius, and Lobelius laid a foundation for modern botany. None were natives of Antwerp—Dodoens came from nearby Mechlin, Lobelius from Flanders, and Clusius from Arras in the French Netherlands. It was the opportunity to publish and the cultural and scholarly circle around Plantin and Ortelius that drew them to Antwerp and its affairs.

Dodoens (1517–85) was the first Belgian botanist to achieve a world-wide reputation. He became interested in botany through medicine, having been trained in medicine at Louvain and at various schools in France, Italy, and Germany. In his first medical publication, he insisted that medical science could not make appreciable advances without a greater emphasis on anatomy and autopsies.

This book (Basle, 1546) was followed in 1548 by a study

on cosmography and astronomy, first printed by Jan van der Loe of Antwerp and later reprinted by Plantin. From 1548 to 1574, when Dodoens was town physician at Mechlin, he made some synoptic tables in physiology, which were printed in 1581. During those years his interest in botany as an adjunct to medicine increased. He took his first big step when his friend and printer, van der Loe, persuaded him to write, in Flemish, a history of plants, which van der Loe in 1554 brought out under the title *Cruydeboeck in den welcken de gheheele historia* . . . . Three years later he printed a French translation by Clusius. The *Cruydeboeck* is not, as some critics say, a translation of Fuchs's herbal, although Dodoens took Fuchs as his model in describing plants. Among other differences, Dodoens's work included information on a number of Low Country plants with which Fuchs would not have been familiar.

The English edition by Henry Lyte was printed in Antwerp and was beautifully illustrated, but 516 out of 870 illustrations were from Fuchs's herbal. Plantin offered to bring out a modified version with new plates, and Dodoens accepted. The work appeared in 1574, the first year of Dodoens's nine long years of exile.

By 1583 he was back in Antwerp at Plantin's helping steer through the press his monumental *History of Plants* in six volumes. This, the famous *Stirpium historae pemptades* (1583), was dedicated to the magistrates of Antwerp. It grouped the known vegetables, flowers, trees, and other flora into classes. Volume 3 treated medicinal herbs, and Volume 2 is a gardener's delight.

Soon he was forced to flee from Antwerp once more, and he ended his days at the University of Leiden as professor of medicine, where he taught pathology, general medicine, and internal diseases. He had planned to do a treatise on gout, but died in 1585 before he could put his thoughts on paper.

Dodoens supplied "the bones so to speak" for many subsequent herbals, and the *Pemptades* made significant contributions; but as Professor A. Wolf points out, "The greatest botanist of the modern era was Clusius, or l'Eclus, of Antwerp (1525–1609)," who supplied much of the flesh. Actually Jules-Charles de Lécluse, or Clusius, belongs to Europe, although both Leiden and Antwerp have a claim on him. For many years the latter city was his intellectual headquarters. Most of his writings were published there by Plantin and Moretus, and the rest at Leiden by Raphelengius. At the University of Leiden he was made honorary professor of botany, a post he held from 1593 until his death in 1609. More important, he was at Leiden when the Hortus Academicus (the University Botanical Garden) was being developed. Clusius was largely responsible for the world-wide fame it subsequently achieved, having through friends and other means provided necessary seeds for it and carefully supervised their planting.

Like Dodoens, Clusius was a physician, but his interest in botany exceeded that of both Dodoens and Lobelius. His chief medical contributions were in pharmacology, in which area he translated a number of books outlining various herb cures. It has been estimated that he added six hundred items to the list of plants known in his day. Best known are the jonquil (*Narcissus jonquilla*)—which he found in the fields near Toledo, Seville, and Cádiz—and the *Narcissus tazetta*, which he came upon at Gibraltar and in Portugal. His two best works are the Historia *stirpium Hispanias* (1576) and the *Historia stirpium Pannonian* (1583)—one the fruits of a tour of the Iberian Peninsula, and the other of a tour of Hungary and Austria, particularly the mountainous areas. Both are systematic and descriptive, and are pioneer works in botanical classification. Later in life he did a study of exotic plants found in the East and West Indies, and his *Fungorum historia* ranks him —unwittingly on his part—as the founder of mycology. He also wrote and translated histories and travel accounts, and conversed with Sir Francis Drake and other renowned mariners about the natural history of the New World.

Plantin in 1601 brought forth an edition of his work which included for the first time in any botanical study a scientific description and illustration of the potato—the tuber that was to revolutionize the dietary habits of Europe. Other European gardens, in addition to the one at Leiden, were enhanced by his labors. Well he deserves the title: *"le père de tous les beaux jardins de ce pays* [the Netherlands]" ("the father of all the beautiful gardens of the Netherlands"). This title could be broadened to include a large part of Europe.

The third member of the triumvirate, Matthias de Lobelius (1538–1616), was closely associated with English gardening. A student of medicine like the other three, he published in England (1569–70), with Pierre Pena, *Stirpium adversaria nova*. Although the work, especially Pena's part, is strictly *materia medica*, it is nonetheless important in the annals of English herbals, because Lobelius introduced, roughly, a separation of the classes called Dicotyledones and Monocotyledones. Lobelius saw a natural kinship among different plants and made natural groupings of grasses, lilies, and orchids. He used the leaf as the basis of classification, and his arrangements are superior to those of Clusius and Dodoens. The flower Lobelia bears his name.

He went to Antwerp immediately after the publication of *Adversaria*, and Plantin brought out an enlarged edition of the work. In 1581 a Flemish translation appeared, the *Krudytboek*, which was dedicated to William the Silent, the burgomasters, and other city dignitaries, and which used Clusius's blocks. Later Plantin published an album of the engravings grouped according to Lobelius's arrangement, now recognized as superior.

Lobelius became private physician to William the Silent, and after William's assassination became town physician in Antwerp. With the triumph of Catholicism, he withdrew to England, where he was private physician to Sir Edward Zouch and royal gardener to James I. He was well received in England and enjoyed harmonious relations with all his fellow herbalists with the exception of Gerard, whom he accused of plagiarism.

Just as the engraver's needle was vital to the herbalist, so it was to the cartographer. Antwerp's great age coincided with the age when mapmakers flourished, and sixteenth-century Europe turned to this city for its maps, globes, and navigation instruments. The city accounts (1504/5) show that a sum of fourteen livres was paid to the illustrator Pieter Borcht for the design of a roller map showing views of the Hondt, the Scheldt, and the rivers of Brabant—all with definitely marked navigation routes. By 1516 the illustrious Liefrinck family had settled in Antwerp. Guillaume was enrolled in Saint Lucas's Guild as a master engraver and numbered among his pupils Sylvester of Paris (1528), Hannekin Molyns (1532), and Lieven Dyck (1538). His son Jean followed in his father's craft as did his daughter Mijnken, who must surely be one of the first female map-engravers. Plantin used the work of Jean for illustrations, and Ortelius used them for reference.

Hans Hogenberg was at Mechlin by 1520, but had close connections in Antwerp; in 1526, Jean de Beeldensnijder of Antwerp published a map of the Baltic. The latter, who limited his maps to Europe, showed artistic talent with elegant frames, gracious escutcheons, and hand-done illuminations.

The desire for good maps was initially more practical than aesthetic. The expanding economy created demands for accurate land routes through Europe and charts for the newly discovered seas. Towns demanded stricter fortification plans. Moreover, the shift from the medieval village to the estate, the enclosure of common lands, and the far-reaching social changes resulting from the Reformation created a need for newer surveying methods and for estate maps. Soon maps began to be valued for their aesthetic qualities, and wall maps in paintings of Low Country interiors verify the appeal of maps for art's sake.

By the end of the sixteenth century, mapmaking had become a highly lucrative business, and superior Flemish instruments, Flemish methods (especially in triangulation), and Flemish craftsmen had in the main replaced those of Italy, Switzerland, and Germany. Plantin was by far the most prolific publisher of atlases, and, with Ortelius and others, formed a group of mapmakers and geographers unrivaled in Europe. The maps they turned out are even today cause for wonderment, for their accuracy as well as for their decorative cartouches, ornamentations and illustrations.

Allied with—indeed, the mother of—cartography was geography. Jan van Doesborch, who may have taken over the printing establishment of Roland van der Dorp, early recognized that a market for geography books existed. In 1506 he brought out in Antwerp *Van Pape Jans landendes*

("The Lands of Pester John"), and in the next year *Van den nieuwer werelt* ("Of the New Lands"), which included a Dutch translation of a letter sent by Amerigo Vespucci to Leonardo de Medici. More significant was the publication in 1508 of *Die reyse van Lissebone* ("The Trip from Lisbon"), an account of a trip from Lisbon to India at the request of Emanual I, king of Portugal. About 1520, Doesborch printed at London an edition of *Of the New Landes*, which his pupil Laurient Andrews probably published from a nonextant Dutch version published earlier by Doesborch. Not only is it the first book on America, but the term "America" is used in English for the first time.

The founder of the Belgian school of cartography was Gemma Frisius (1508–55), who originally came from Groningen but who spent his most productive years at Louvain. His reputation was established in 1529 when he published the *Cosmographie* of the German Phillipus Aprianus. At twenty-two, Frisius was teaching cosmography to young Gerhard Kremer, or Mercator (1512–94). In 1523 he brought forth *Een boecxken seer nut ende profitelijck allen geographiens* ... ("A Book Very Useful and Profitable for All Geographers"). All works by Frisius except for a map of the world were published in Antwerp. In *De usu globi* (1530), Frisius described a way to calculate longitude which preceded John Harrison by two hundred years. He invented an instrument by which he could tell time in all parts of the world, improved the astrolabe, and, most important of all, inspired Mercator.

That worthy was born in Rupelmonde, a city in East Flanders. From there he went to the University of Louvain to Frisius. By 1532 he moved to Antwerp where he continued his studies in mathematics, astronomy, and other subjects allied with cosmology. Frisius and the university

were sufficiently close for books, ideas, and encouragement, and, at Antwerp, he was able to meet foreign merchants, a real advantage to the geographer. In workaday
Antwerp, he practiced applied science. He learned engraving and perfected his craft in making globes, astrolabes, and
astronomical rings. He supported himself by surveying,
laying out building plots, and making drawings of buildings. He married an Antwerp girl, whose father was financial officer at Louvain, and he returned to the university in
1534.

The oldest known map produced by Mercator was one
of Palestine (1537), followed the next year by his first map
of the world. Coincidental with the map of the Holy Land
was a treatise by Mercator on the Creation. His world map
was made with the famous Mercator projection in which
the sphericity of the earth was taken into account and
allowed for a varying scale at the equator and at the poles.
In 1564 the map of the British Isles appeared, to be followed
five years later by the famous world map of twenty-four
pages entitled *Nova et aucta orbis terrai descriptio ad usum
navigatium emendate accomodata*. His studies in magnetism
helped place more accurately the line of no compass devi-
ation.

Mercator in 1540 drew a map of Flanders for a group of
merchants, presumably Antwerpians, and recommended
that Latin cursive script be used in the titling of maps. At
the same time he brought forth a terrestrial globe, followed
in ten years by an astronomical one.

In 1552 he went to Duisburg for religious reasons. There
he produced an atlas of Europe, globes, and other maps. In
addition, he wrote books of instruction for the use of his
own globes and astronomical ferrules. From about 1570 to
his death, he allowed his sons and grandsons to begin to

take over the chores of engraving. Throughout his years at Duisburg, he was a faithful correspondent of Plantin and Ortelius.

From his study he kept abreast of the latest travel accounts. He modified his conceptions of Africa after the observations of the Portuguese explorers Bartholomeo Diaz and Vasco da Gama, and his later maps of North America show it separated from Asia. On the other hand, his maps indicated a northwest passage to the Orient.

Today the efforts of Mercator are recognized as paramount in the field of sixteenth-century cartography, but at the time, to the general public, Abraham Ortelius (1527–98) was the shining light in the discipline. Called by one writer "the complete Antwerpian," Ortelius from his native city, which presented him with the "wine of honour," firmly established the reputation of the Netherlands as a center for the production and publication of maps.

Mercator inspired and encouraged him, and he brought out in 1570 the *Theatrum orbis terrarum*. R. V. Tooley commented in *Maps and Map-Makers*: "The publication of this atlas marked an epoch in the history of cartography. It was the first uniformly sized, systematic collection of maps in the countries of the world based only on contemporary knowledge since the days of Ptolemy and in that sense may be called the first modern atlas."

The *Theatrum* is a tribute to the scholarship and unselfishness of many men. Mercator may have conceived the idea, but Ortelius supplied Mercator with information. Mercator caused Ortelius to be less the dilettante, less the publisher, and more the scientist. Ortelius assembled, amassed, and formulated the collection; Mercator elaborated and organized it.

Others assisted, among them March Laurén, who did the

topography of Biervliet; Martin de Vos, who was consulted on the ornamentation so important in productions by the Flemish school; Gilles Hooftman, the financial director of the project; Gilles Coppens, who printed and sold the edition; the Plantin workshop that assisted in making the engravings, but not as much as Abraham Verhoeven and Mijnken Liefrinck; Ferdinand and Ambroise Arsenius, grandsons of Frisius, who printed the world map; and Jean Surhon, Chrétien Sgroot, and Egide Bulonius, who did important individual maps. The one notable omission was Gérard de Jode's map of Scandinavia.

The *Theatrum*, which popularized the study of geography and went through a number of editions, became the model for the Flemish style in cartography, ousting that of the Italians. This style "in the rather too elaborate form given it by the Dutch after the fall of Antwerp . . . prevailed all over Europe right down to about 1700." Although the Italian symbols were preserved, the coloring revived the tradition of the Middle Ages, with blue seas and rivers, green woods, red towns, etc. The borders and cartouches catered to an age that reveled in color. The former were narrower and less prominent, but the latter substituted "strapwork" for a wooden frame around the title filled with every ornamental design that the pattern books could devise. The lettering was Italic; that is, the fine "copper-plate hand which the engravers used and the writing masters taught."

In the eyes of the world, the *Theatrum* was Ortelius's finest achievement. In the field of cartography, his best contribution was an atlas of the Netherlands, and *Germania inferior*, which was done in 1586 and edited by van Vrients in 1603. The bibliographies that Ortelius enclosed with his atlases added little to the knowledge of cartography, but

are valuable because Ortelius, collector that he was, preserved information on the state of geography and cartography of his day which otherwise would have been lost.
His earlier maps showed Lower California to be a peninsula, although editions after his death show it as an island.
His conception of North America, although incorrect,
stimulated Dutch and English explorers to search for northwest and northeast passages. The edition of 1595 shows
rather well the course of the Congo River as verified in the
nineteenth century by Livingstone, Stanley, and others.

Closely associated with Ortelius was the cartographer
and linguist Arnold van der Mylen, who persuaded Ortelius
to write the *Trésor geographique*, in which geographical
and other terms of the ancients were translated into modern
phraseology. Ortelius also befriended Pieter Heyns and
commissioned him to do a Flemish edition of the *Theatrum*
and an abbreviated version of it suitable for young students.
The engraver Philippe Galle drew the portrait of Ortelius
found in the *Theatrum* and a series of prints for Heyns's
Epitome. Frans Hogenberg, friend to both Mercator and
Ortelius, conceived from the *Theatrum* the idea of the
Civitas orbis terrarum, still the most magnificent of all city
atlases, which he did with Georg Braun, with help from
Joris Hoefnagel. All but the first volume was done outside
Antwerp, however, because Braun, a German visitor, and
Hogenberg were forced to flee. Ortelius collected views
and plans for them and assisted them in other ways to com-
pile the *Civitas*, which at the time was considered a supplement to the *Theatrum*. In the making of maps, the plan of
Antwerp by Virgilius Poloniensis and Cornelis Graphaeus
(1565) is an outstanding extant example of sixteenth-century Flemish cartography.

Like Hogenberg, many eminent cartographers had to

flee Antwerp and the surrounding countryside in the face of religious persecution. The list is formidable. Mercator and son Rumoldus, Orteleanus, Jodicus Hondius, Pieter Heyns, and Philippe Galle are only a few. Many were successful in their new homes. Guillaume Tavernier, for example, was so well received in Paris that his son who carried on the business was raised to the rank of baron by Louis XIV. With most of those cartographers, Ortelius remained in close communication, and he often helped them financially.

Outside the brilliant circle of Ortelius was the de Jode family. Ortelius avoided them perhaps because he was jealous of old Gérard, or perhaps because the family originally had been Jewish. The latter reason seems to fall short, however, because there was a time when Gérard de Jode (1515–91) and Ortelius apparently had a cordial relationship. Gérard in 1547 entered Saint Lucas Guild as an "engraver and print seller," the same year that Ortelius was enscribed as an "illuminator of maps."

Gérard came from an artistic Nijmegen family and by 1555 had cut a number of engravings, aided in his work by the brothers Jean and Lucas Deutecum. The works were extremely well done, and Gérard soon became one of the most popular map engravers in Antwerp. A map of France, *Amplissima tabula Galliae*, appeared in about 1568, followed closely by an important collection of German maps in which Gérard showed the courses of the Rhine and Danube plus all the important overland routes.

This latter work anticipated the *Theatrum*, but the maps, designed to be detached and sold separately, had no systematic organization. De Jode and Ortelius not only went often to the same sources but at times employed the same engravers. The only instance, however, in which Ortelius cited de Jode was apropos of a map of Sweden by Lievin Algoet. The two changed plates in subsequent editions, but Ortelius, having government privilege, was protected from plagiarism, and de Jode was not. Gérard was not equal to Mercator in scientific knowledge; indeed, he had a poor conception of Mercator's projection. He did, however, rival Ortelius as an editor and engraver of maps. His *Speculum orbis terrae* is one of the very rare and far too often ignored works in the history of cartography. Of passing interest is that Gérard did a man's head designed by Adrianus Hubertus, illustrating the functioning of the five senses, which precluded a system of craniology made famous in the eighteenth century by Dr. Ball of Baden.

Gérard's son, Corneille (1568–1600), united in a single volume the works of his father and a world map (*Mappemonde*) of his own. He utilized a severe Mercator-type projection and employed as decorator the gifted Antoine Wiericx, who was employed by Corneille on other projects. Corneille included accompanying texts, and his *Indroductio geographica* . . . (1595) contains information about Central Africa, especially about the great interior, which was not "discovered" until the nineteenth century.

The last outstanding geographer to be considered in this chapter is Ludovico Guicciardini (1521–89) who has been so often quoted in previous pages. Although he was a Florentine and nephew of the celebrated Francesco Guicciardini, he is more closely identified with the Low Countries than with his native Italy. As Louis Wauwermans put it: "Louis Guicciardini (Lodovico Guicciardini) contemporary friend of Ortelius, foreigner but naturalized by a long stay in Belgium, perhaps may legitimately be considered as a representative of *the Flemish* school with whom he complemented *works in cartography* by remarkable *literary descriptions* which in general were lacking in this school."

Raised in an atmosphere where intellectual activity was held in high esteem and trade and commerce were not despised, he was sent on business to Antwerp, where a similar balance between trade and the intellect prevailed. The exact date of his arrival in Antwerp is not known, but he was active there in 1542. His brother Giovanni did a *Mappemonde* in 1549 and was among those consulted by Ortelius about the form most suitable for the *Theatrum*.

Ludovico cultivated his own intellectual tastes. He collected maxims by various authors under the title *Ore da recreasione* ("Recreational Hours"), which were printed in Venice in 1567 and reprinted the same year in Antwerp by Willem Sylvius. A more important book done during the same period covered events in Europe from the Treaty of Cambrai (1520) to 1560. Entitled *Commentarii delle cosse più memorabile*, it was printed in both Venice and Antwerp in 1566.

His next work, a description of Antwerp, had an enthusiastic reception. He dedicated it to the town magistrates and claimed to have written the book not only to show to the world the "beauty, grandeur, and magnificence" of the city, but also to illustrate the "great affection he held for it." The favorable reaction to the *Antwerp* caused him to write a description of the Low Countries, as Leandro Alberti had done for Italy. *The Descrittione di tutte paesibassi attrement; detti germani inferiore*, dedicated to Philip II, came from the press of Sylvius in 1567. In the same year the publisher brought out a French translation of the work dedicated to Margaret of Austria.

While writing the book, Guicciardini consulted the most learned authorities of his day, among them his friend Pieter

Heyns, whom he considered to be an "affable savant and good poet." Ortelius furnished him with maps for the study of Brabant, Friesland, Holland, Zeeland, Utrecht, and Flanders. C. de Hooge, self-styled bastard of Charles V, and Philippe Galle supplied the illustrations.

The *Description* occupies an important place in Flemish geography. Admittedly it is weak on the discussion of soils and their chemical components, and the waterways. In some respects it is a travel account written to satisfy the curiosity of the tourist and the needs of the merchant. It is, however, more than that. Guicciardini was hardly a traveler, living for years as he did in a large beautiful house on the rue du Marquis. He was a resident observer with a keen eye, and his work demands a first rank in descriptive geography.

Plantin published the second edition of the *Description*, and a French edition appeared in 1582. In the meantime Cornelis Kiel had finished a translation of the work into Flemish, which was published with new engravings in 1581. Guicciardini addressed a complimentary copy "to the illustrious magistrates of Antwerp" as an acknowledgment of the hospitality he had enjoyed in the city. In return the town fathers in a solemn ceremony on March 6, 1581, placed a golden chain around the neck of Guicciardini, Italian-born but now full-fledged Antwerpian.

As a citizen, he had witnessed the excesses of the Iconoclasts, the persecutions of Alva, and the Spanish Fury. Always he remained faithful to Antwerp, the city in whose future he believed and in whose cruel adventures he shared. He was completely associated with the Netherlands cause, but being an Italian, he was viewed with distrust. Because of trade associates, he was suspected in 1582 of being implicated in an attempt to assassinate William of Orange, and for several months was held in custody. The incident left a bitter taste in his mouth, but he still assisted the city in its defense against Parma. He died on March 23, 1587. His final resting place fittingly was the adopted land he had loved and had so vividly described.

CHAPTER VII

"Merchandise of no little importance"

Sixteenth-century Antwerp was a city of Renaissance men—versatile, many-sided, and impossible to categorize. Composers were at times music publishers and editors. The engraver could be a hired hand to trace a leaf for a herbal or to illustrate a globe. The cartographer could be engraver, geographer, and businessman; the poet, a city official. Since the historian for the sake of order and clarity sometimes must create categories, however, artists are here treated apart from engravers and musicians apart from poets, even when they are the same individuals.

Antwerp engravers had achieved supremacy over the Italians by the end of the sixteenth century, and, along with Amsterdam engravers (which included Europe's greatest needlist, Rembrandt van Rijn), were to maintain that superiority during much of the next hundred years: So long as Antwerp remained Europe's printing center, the best engravers would be attracted to the city. For nearly two hundred years, painting, practiced by such masters as Massys, Floris, and Pieter Brueghel the elder, was of vital significance there, and the works of Antwerp's artists and engravers commanded a market throughout Europe, constituting, in Guicciardini's words, "merchandise of no little importance."

In 1565, with an ever-increasing demand for emblems, portraits, and book illustrations, Flemish engravers were producing every sort of print. "From Antwerp especially the output was enormous: engravings of paintings and of maps, portraits, illustrations and decorative borders for books were turned out in huge quantities. Flemish books of patterns were used by English craftsmen and Flemish plates by English printers." There was a demand for such art work in other parts of Europe as well, increased during the Indian summer of Antwerp's decline. During the latter period the Sadeleer family of Brussels had branches in Prague and Vienna, Dominicus Custos of Antwerp had settled in Augsburg, and the great Antwerp houses of Cock, Galle, and van de Passe were setting high standards in Flemish-style engravings throughout Europe. The Catholic Jesuit press at Antwerp employed the Wiericx brothers to manufacture visual aids to help bring the wayward back to Christ.

Admittedly the best engravings in the Plantin Museum were ordered after 1585 by Plantin's successors, who were contemporaries of the best of the Flemish craftsmen. Yet Plantin himself set the standard. As he said: "I have never neglected when I had the opportunity and the ability to pay for the work of the best engravers." He loved a beautiful book, and after his accident, "What he could not do on book covers with gilding-tools, he tried to have done on the printed leaves from wood-cuts from designs by eminent artists."

Plantin increasingly used engravings in wood. The woodcuts used in the herbals of Dodoens would today be regarded as extravagant. "To this day they are models of good line drawing and clean engraving. When the text did not call for descriptive illustrations, he made free use of large initial head-bands and tail-pieces. The shelves and closets of the Museum contain thousands of initials remarkable for the vigor of their designs or the ingenuity of their backgrounds or 'interlacings.' One series is about five inches square." Plantin later moved to copper plates. The *Huna-mae salutes monumenta* of 1571, with seventy-one large plates, was his earliest and most noteworthy example.

Plantin paid four to seven sous for the design of a beautiful initial letter. C. van den Broeck received six florins for a full-page design of "Our Lady of Seven Sorrows," and the dissolute but talented Jerome Wiericx was paid ninety-six florins for doing a superb engraving of van den Broeck's design. The usual price demanded by the brothers Wiericx was thirty florins to engrave a plate of folio size. Some other renowned engravers associated with Plantin were P. van der Borcht, Lucas de Heere, Godfrey Ballain, Martin de Vos, P. Huys, A. de Bruyn, J. Sadeleer, Jan Meyssens, P. Galle, Christoffel Jegher, and many more.

Nicholas de Bruyn and Léonard Terwoort had noteworthy and successful careers as engravers after they left Antwerp. The former settled in Amsterdam, where he patterned many of his engravings on the style of Lucas van Leyden. Terwoort moved to London, where he worked on the *Atlas* of Christopher Saxton. His lettering was in a flowery hand "with delightful capitals and flourishes," and his cartouches "are certainly the largest and most fantastic that the Flemish-English school ever put on a map." To a menagerie of birds and animals he added what became on the Dutch maps of the next century a stereotyped and very annoying feature: simpering cupids or cherubs clambering all over the cartouche and the scale.

Hieronymous Cock, son of the talented painter Jean Willem Cock, was held in higher esteem during his own lifetime than he is today. He was born in Antwerp in 1510, studied there under François de Vriendt, and became a

master in the Saint Lucas Guild in 1545. After an extended
stay in Italy, he established himself in 1553 at the "Quatre
Vents" on Exchange Street as an engraver. Hieronymous
habitually placed pithy sayings on his engravings containing plays on the word "Cock." For example one such line
reads *Houdt de cocq in eeien* ("Hold the cock in high
esteem"). His fine engravings of the Antwerp fortifications
built by Charles V are all signed H.C.F. (Hieronymous
Cock *fecit*).

It was Coeck van Aalst (1502–50), the painter and engraver, who pioneered the spread of Renaissance artistic
ideas into Flemish architecture. Although early in his career
he wrote a sixty-four-page book on architecture, he is
remembered primarily for translating into Netherlands the
architectural studies of Sebastiano Serlio based on Vitruvius. The work is more than a translation. At times he used
Serlio; at times he did not. He also provided illustrations and
made commentaries on the text. It is the first architectural
handbook in the Netherlands tongue and was designed to
give practical assistance to builders, painters, sculptors, and
wood carvers.

Van Aalst promoted the classical style, and his own hand
is very much in evidence in later editions of the work. This
is especially noticeable in the woodcuts incorporated into
English, French, German, and Dutch editions. By way of
illustration, Vredeman de Vries came to understand Serlio
through Coeck, whose ideas he used after he left Antwerp
for Amsterdam. Robert Peake, the royal painter of James
I who translated Serlio's five books from Netherlands into
English, also owed Coeck van Aalst an immeasurable debt.
As Guicciardini said, Coeck "transported to the Low Countries the true practice of architecture."

If the Renaissance style was "transplanted" by Coeck van

Aalst, it was grafted onto a native Flemish stock by Vrede-man de Vries before the hybrid seedlings were exported to much of northern Europe. De Vries, as his name implies, was born in Friesland. After studying painting in Amsterdam under Reyer Cerritsen, he moved to Antwerp and remained in the Antwerp-Mechlin area from 1547 to about 1570. An ardent Calvinist, he was in exile for five years but returned to Antwerp in 1575 when the Protestant cause was at its peak. Soon the ebb began. He helped plan the defenses of the city against Parma, but to no avail. When the city fell, Vredeman once more took up his travels, working in Frankfurt, Danzig, Hamburg, and Amsterdam, where he died in 1606.

His influence on architecture continued well up to the end of the seventeenth century. The impact of the Antwerp City Hall—which he designed and Cornelis de Vrient built—on the subsequent design of municipal buildings elsewhere in Europe "was largely due to the inexhaustible inventiveness" of Vredeman, whose collections of designs with varying cartouches and grotesques were against the purely classical taste of the early Flemish Renaissance. Attempts to combine native tradition with that of the Italians reached their culmination in this structure in which Vredeman replaced "the cheerful and delicate chasteness" of the classical with "a certain heavy luxurious exuberance." He put classical window pediments in a brick façade with pointed or stepped gables. Those same steps he embellished with statuary and cartouche work, the abomination of the classical purist, exemplifying the tenacious resistance of Flemish tradition to the Italianate style. With this building Vredeman "did great service in preparing the way for the really brilliant, if brief, period of Netherlandish architecture . . . ."

His legacy which has endured best, however, is printed on paper rather than engraved on stone, his writings having weathered time better than the City Hall and his other architectural creations. His plan and pattern books influenced such buildings as the City Hall in Danzig and Wollaton House in England. They include almost every type of design from costume to furniture. Gérard de Jode published the *Cartels* in 1555, a book of Vredeman cartouches with twelve plates. Throughout the rest of his life, Vredeman continued to devise designs and publish them. Some of the best engravers of the day did his plates: de Jode, H. Cock, P. Galle, and later J. Janssonius. Special patterns were designed for makers of vases, gravestones, and other objects.

The best known of his works, the *Architectura*, may have appeared as early as 1565. A better edition was brought out in 1577, and between 1581 and 1589 it was translated into Netherlands, Latin, and French. The last edition to be completed in his lifetime was done with his son Paul, and was printed at The Hague in 1606. The *Architectura* discusses five orders of columns and supplies building hints for façades, household furnishings, canals, locks, bridges, and other structures. Vredeman gave credit to Vitruvius, but insisted that what was right, proper, and functional in antiquity might be gauche in the sixteenth and seventeenth centuries.

Vredeman's *Perspective* followed a similar course. The most interesting edition is perhaps the 1599 one by Hondius, because it contains a picture of Vredeman, who was seventy-seven at the time. This delightful old book provides instruction in perspective drawing and contains magnificent illustrations of vaultings, decorated arches, pendants, swags, nymphs, shields, heads, strapwork, and façades. Also included are instructions for designing rooms, bedchambers, galleries, gardens, streets, and even alleys. No matter what the problem, Vredeman's solution contained a mixture of the Flemish traditional, the antique, and a jarring and incoherent profusion of detail.

Vredeman was not the only designer whose pattern books had an international market. Abraham de Bruyn and his son Nicholas, like Vredeman and his son Paul, were active in both Antwerp and Amsterdam and were highly influential. Emblem books were also being engraved and published in Antwerp at this time. Octavus van Veen, teacher of Rubens, instilled in his pupil love of classical antiquity. He illustrated Horace with emblems in 1607, and the next year with *Amorum emblemata* "drew upon the father of erotic concerts, Ovid, in order to translate his lines into pictures." In *Amoris divini emblemata* (1615) he substituted Saint Augustine for Ovid.

During its years of glory, Antwerp served the ear as well as the eye. Guicciardini observed that "One can see at almost every hour of the day weddings, dancing, and musical groups. There is hardly a corner of the streets not filled with the joyous sounds of instrumental music and singing." F. Pourbus (1545–81) portrays a wedding of a fellow artist, Hoefnagel, at which a clavichord was played; J. van Oost the elder (1601–71) painted a musical soiree with violins and a cello. David Teniers (1610–90) in *Vlaamse kermis* contrasted the musical tastes of the upper class enjoying a stately dance with the jigging of the country people. Another painting by Pourbus shows an intimate ensemble playing lutes, flutes, and recorders and accompanying the music with eating, drinking, and flirting. Guicciardini summed it up well: "The Belgians are indeed true masters and restorers of music; they have studied it and reduced it to perfection . . . having men and women sing without learning, but with a real instinct for tone and measure; also they use instruments of all sorts which everyone understands and knows."

Music was not reserved to a single class. Weddings, banquets, balls, serenades, morning band concerts by the military, masques, theatrical performances, *ommegangen* (religious processions), civic festivals, baptisms, masses, and Joyous Entries were rarely without music. In music, as in other branches of culture, Antwerp enjoyed a position not rivaled elsewhere in Europe. A corps of musicians daily escorted the delegates of the Hanseatic League as they went from their factory to the Bourse to occupy themselves with mundane matters of commerce. In the midst of such pleasures and prodigalities, musicians were sought after.

Many instrumentalists were attracted to Antwerp from France, Italy, Germany, and other cities in the Low Countries. Here the highly cultivated burgher society assured them of a livelihood. The city itself supported five musicians, among them Tielman Susato, and paid a fixed sum of money to musicians participating in the *ommegangen*. The artists in turn hired their own helpers—often apprentice musicians who boarded with them for a price agreed upon by the parents and who were expected to supply their own instruments.

Musicians at times organized themselves into associations (*benden*). The members of such groups were music teachers as well as performers. Those persons desiring musical services negotiated with the head of the association, who set the fees and decided which instruments would be used, the number of musicians needed, and other details. One such association was headed by Georges Lohoys of Rique-bourg and Jean Hobreau of Douai.

The two went into partnership March 20, 1541. They swore before the magistrates that they would use the talents God had given them for the well-being of the com-munity. They promised to play at all usual affairs and accept other engagements whenever they had openings. They pledged not to make double bookings, or to cut short performances. They agreed to instruct apprentices in all instruments "expected of them by the laws of the town," and to teach dancing publicly and privately to young and old. They were to receive reasonable fees for their efforts, from which Lohoys, the better established, would keep the larger percentage.

There were many other "professors" of music who made comfortable livings teaching or performing in the various musical events which took place in the city. Many of these *facteurs de clavecins* or *chanteurs* are nameless, but they reflected musical tastes. Guicciardini does mention two by the names Catherine and Christian, "who played the espenettes and other instruments" so well that the Queen of Hungary left them a lifetime legacy in her will.

The Church, as might be expected, attracted the best musicians. Dürer was amazed at the musical excellence found in the Church of Our Lady, where at one time he saw two masses being sung at once. What really impressed the German artist was that in addition to the main choir there were three other jubes (rood lofts) in the church, each having its own organ, master of music, musicians, and organist distinct from those of the main choir.

Needless to say, the Church musicians were famous throughout Europe as performers, composers, teachers, choirmasters, and sometimes music printers. Four of the most important of these in Antwerp were Antoine Barbé, master of the Chapel of the Collegiants of Saint Mary's; Tielman Susato, chief of Antwerp's town musicians, editor and corrector (*correcteur*) of music; Hubert Waelrant, learned theorist, singer, teacher, composer, and music editor; and Orlande de Lassus, who spent two years in Antwerp—where the Susato publishing house brought out his first group of French and Italian songs—before leaving to direct the choir of the duke of Bavaria.

Barbé was called to Antwerp in 1527 to succeed Master Nicolle as master of music for Our Lady's Church and for all of its jubes. While he was music master (1527–62), Barbé wrote a large number of religious chants, masses, motets, hymns, anthems, and magnificats. The manuscript copies of his works were destroyed with the compositions of many others in 1566 when the Iconoclasts ransacked the church library. Fortunately for posterity, some of his works had been printed by Tielman Susato and W. van Vissenaaecken. During the years he was choirmaster, he made Antwerp a European musical center. Barbé's son, Antoine II, and his grandson, Antoine III, were accomplished musicians and organists at the Church of Saint Walburg and the Church of Saint James, respectively. Antoine III wrote an excellent treatise on musical tones that was published in Antwerp in 1599.

Gerard de Turnhout (1520–80) succeeded Barbé at Our Lady's. He had entered orders in 1562 and the next year became music master for the Confrérie of the Virgin at Our Lady's and chaplain for the chantries on the right side of the choir. The same year (1563) he took over Barbé's position and in 1564 composed a *Te Deum* for the entry of Margaret of Parma into Antwerp. From 1567 to 1568 he

labored with infinite care and patience putting back together the broken pieces left by the vandals of 1566. The
music library had been burned and the organs smashed.

He composed masses, motets, and chansons for from two
to ten voices. His *Fleur des chansons* was highly popular
in his own day. His Flemish songs in *Een Duytsch musyck
boek* (Louvain, 1572) are perhaps the most interesting.
They are highly joyous, and one of his best lyrics has the
simple title "My Heart Recommends Itself to You."
Phalèse and Susato were his publishers, the former having
shops in both Antwerp and Brussels. His son Jean (1550–
1611) was a composer of considerable talent, and from
1586 on was master of the chapel of the duke of Parma.
Some of his works were published in Antwerp.

Séverin Cornet succeeded Turnhout to the mastership of
the Cathedral choir. Cornet was an especially fine teacher
who wielded considerable influence over the young, one
of his best pupils being Corneille Verdonck (1563–1625).
Plantin published five music books by Cornet, and in 1581
brought out three of them with Latin, French, and Italian
texts.

Now, as in his own time, Tielman Susato is more highly
revered than Cornet. Susato was born in Cologne, but by
1529 he was well established in Antwerp, and he died there
in 1561. He was an instrumentalist and music copier as
well as a composer, but his primary job was printing music.
The age demanded songbooks for voice and instruments,
and the ready market made music publishing profitable.
Susato between 1543 and 1561 printed over fifty volumes
of music. So popular were music books that the Church of
Saint James in 1575 held a lottery in which the prizes were
copies of a songbook published by Gilles van den Rade and
entitled *Dieurscher refereynen* (Antwerp, 1574). The "di-

verse songs" were taken from productions by various chambers, and the lottery was announced in a pamphlet containing a jingle not much different from a television commercial. One likes to speculate on whether the jingle itself was set to music.

In 1530, Susato transcribed a massive book of music (thirty-three volumes in six parts), which ran to about four hundred folio pages. The next year he was admitted to the corps of city musicians (*stadsspeellieden*), but lost that post for some unknown reason in 1549 when Philip II arrived. Already he had become a music publisher.

His first book of songs, *Chansons* (1543), had ten authors, but Susato himself wrote eight songs, which included some dances extremely lively and excellently written. It was the first collection of polyphonic chansons printed in the Low Countries. He wrote four additional music books. The fourth included a number of *Souterliedekens* ("Psalm ditties") written by Jacques Clemens non Papa, one of the most renowned musicians of the century. The third, *Musyck boexken*, was the first songbook in the Netherlands language to be printed in the Low Countries. The four books have another interesting feature: The parts for the instruments are not the same as those written for the voices. Furthermore, Susato's use of rhythm and his structure are in places quite different from the vocal polyphony of the age. His son Jacques continued the family tradition and in 1564 published a collection of four-part songs, twenty-seven of them done by Orlande de Lassus. Father and son both used Italian capitals in their works, an innovation in Flemish music printing; and both printed the musical characters on five lines, imitating the Parisian printer, Pierre Hautin. Among the musicians for whom Susato published, in addition to Clemens non Papa, were Thomas Créquillon,

Nicolas Gombert, Claude Goudimel, Orlande de Lassus, Pierre de Manchicourt, Jean Mouton, Cyprien de Rore, and Adrian Willaert.

During his lifetime, Susato wrote at least thirty-eight songs, thirty of them profane and the others religious. In composition he showed independence and originality, especially in part writing, an art in which he was so proficient that some of his three part songs are composed in such a manner as to be equally suitable for three voices and for two, with the omission of the bass. He collaborated with non Papa in some compositions and published some of non Papa's works, probably while non Papa was working in the Antwerp Cathedral, before he left to become choir-master in Vienna.

Non Papa wrote ten volumes of masses and seven books of motets that were published in Louvain by Phalèse between 1556 and 1560. "He seems to have attempted all the styles then known. He was no slave to counterpoint, but for his time possessed an extraordinary amount of medodies and clear harmony. No one in his day surpassed him for tunefulness and elegance; his medodies are far more fresh and pleasing than those of his contemporaries, and his style is easy, simple, and clear. That he often pushed imitation too far and neglected the true accentuation of the text is only to say he belongs to the 16th century."

The *Souterliedekens* brought non Papa and Susato together. These are pieces from a Flemish rhymed version of the Psalms set without change to current popular tunes. Their charm lies less in the airs adapted than in the independence and originality of the part writing, at which Susato was so expert. The first book of the *Souterliedekens* with monophonic settings had been printed by Simon Cock (Antwerp, 1540), and from that time to 1613 went through thirty-three editions. Non Papa and Susato adapted the texts to part settings, and Jan Fruytiers, the Lutheran poet and musician, used thirty-four of the same melodies for his rhymed version of the *Ecclesiasticus* (Antwerp, 1565). The French poet Clément Marot may have indirectly contributed to the *Souterliedekens* by publishing the Psalms at Antwerp prior to 1540. While he was in Antwerp, he completed the text for the 1541 edition of the Psalms.

The only rival to outdistance the House of Susato in music printing was that of Phalèse. The founder of the dynasty was Pierre the elder (1510–73), who started publishing music at Louvain about 1545. Ten years later he was both printer and publisher. From 1570 on, the firm was associated with Jan Beller in Antwerp, although old Pierre remained at Louvain. Not so the children, who moved to Antwerp. Corneille after a brief career in printing left the firm in the hands of his cadet brother, Pierre the younger, who was inscribed in Antwerp's Saint Lucas Guild in 1581 and was married in the Cathedral the next year. By then he was issuing books at the sign of the Red Lion on the Kammenstraat and in 1608 moved to "De Koning David" on the same street. This shop under the sign of David was under the active guidance of the family until 1674. Pierre the younger had two daughters, Marie and Madeleine, who in 1629 were enrolled in the Guild as "*docters* ('daughters') Phalèse." For over a hundred years the firm was closely identified with European musical history. A catalog of Phalèse publications is an almost complete bibliography of the best in Netherlands music printing.

Although born in Tongerloo about 1517, Hubert Waelrant was closely connected with Antwerp for the greater part of his life and died there in 1595. He published, composed, sang, studied theory, and taught in the music school he founded at Antwerp. He was one of the early musicians in the north to adopt a system of solmization based on the octave rather than the hexachord. He was tenor soloist in the jube of the chapel of the Virgin of Saint Michael's Church, Antwerp. With his partner John Laet he contributed notably to the history of music printing. Between 1554 and 1556 they did five books of motets for five and six voices by various authors. Waelrant's own compositions were included in books 4 and 5. In 1556 they edited three books entitled *Jardin musiqual*, and a book of works by de Lassus, which was dedicated to Cardinal Granvelle. Two years later there appeared a book which consisted primarily of Waelrant's works.

Antwerp exported not only songbooks, compositions, and artists such as Turnhout and Georges de la Héle; it was also one of Europe's main sources of musical instruments. Organs, virginals, harpsichords, spinets, clavichords, "velt-trumpets," oboes, drums, "teneure-pipes," lutes, carillons, violas de gamba—in fact, all known instruments of the day—were manufactured and distributed there. Clavecins were most in demand, and by the early sixteenth century they had superseded the clavichord. The original clavecin was in the shape of a trapeze, but the Venetians soon introduced a clavecin in clavichord shape called a spinet.

As early as 1519, Goosen Kareest (Carest), a pupil of Pieter Mathys, was enrolled as a clavecin maker in Saint Lucas Guild. In 1557 ten clavecin makers were accorded full Guild privileges. The original ten petitioners were protected from imitation by a system whereby each master had his own seal, and apprentices on entering the Guild had to exhibit clavecins "oblong or with bent sides." Soon

Antwerp clavecins were famous. Amsterdam paid two
hundred florins for an Antwerp "clavecimpbel" for its
great organist Jan Pietersz Sweelinck, who took it with him
on all his travels.

The Rucker family made harpsichords in Antwerp from
1579 to 1665. The famous London harpsichord makers,
Kirkman and Shudi, learned their craft from Ruckers. One
hundred years after Rucker instruments were made, renowned artists were commissioned to paint on them. New
jacks and new keys might replace old ones, but so long as
the soundboard stood, the "silvery sweet" tone lasted. It
lasts today.

It was through the painting of clavecins that the instrument makers obtained entry into Saint Lucas Guild. The
Guild had a long history. As early as 1382, the gold- and
silversmiths, the painters, the glassmakers, the embroi-
derers, the wood sculptors, and the enamelers applied to
the magistrates for an association, which became a guild
in 1442. At first the goldsmiths predominated, but by the
fifteenth century the painters had become the most influential group. In 1453 there were only 35 members, but by
1490 the membership was 212. It continued to increase as
the extant register of the Guild (1453–1615) shows. It
possessed its own chapel at Saint Mary's, and a house on
Brewers Street, but in 1505 the members came to occupy
as a hall the floor of the "Fur Cloak" on Market Street. It
was there that Dürer dined—"all their service being of
silver, and they had other splendid ornaments and very
sumptuous meats." In 1530 the Guild took a house on the
Mier called The Tree which the members decorated
magnificently.

In 1460 the chapter built a pand in the churchyard of
Our Lady, where art works were sold until 1540, at which

time the works were moved to shops over the New Bourse. The Pand was the first market in Flanders for pictures. Art works were also sold at the home of the painter or at the Guild Hall. The Guild in 1480 required all vendors to display their works at the market for a period of two years. Only Guild members were allowed to traffic in art works, and each new member of the Guild paid a florin to the Church of Our Lady. Illegitimate children were charged a higher fee. Workmanship was scrutinized closely, and the use of materials was strictly controlled. Careful use of pigment and other materials is one of the reasons Flemish paintings have endured so well through the centuries.

The register of Saint Lucas Guild during the sixteenth century is an almost complete list of north European painters, with some artists from the south thrown in for good measure. About a thousand artists spent some time in Antwerp, having been born there, having learned their trade there, or having resided there during the period. The tremendous number of art pieces turned out by so sizable a group is difficult to visualize. Since many of the works were destroyed by Iconoclasts or Spanish soldiers, the art treasures that went up in smoke can be imagined only from reports by those who saw them. Often all that one has to rely on is a book by the Dutch Vasari, Carel van Mander, who, unfortunately, based much of the material in *Het schilderboek* ("The Book of Painters") on hearsay.

The sixteenth century was an era of transition in Netherlands art. Many critics deprecate the period because of the mannerisms employed by the artists. Max Friedlander complains that the artists were too much swayed by customer demands, and that Antwerp, in which relatively few talented artists were born, lured artists to the city with the promise of silver. Antwerp was indeed a magnet for artists because there they found a favorable climate for their work —association with other artists, a chance to study with the best teachers, an opportunity to make a living from art.

Training of children in art and handicraft created a demand for and an appreciation of art, and undoubtedly influenced the development of the Antwerp school of painting, whose earliest exponent was Jan Snellart. Lucas Cranack, Dürer, Hans Balding Grien, and Lucas van Leyden painted in the city during the first quarter of the sixteenth century and then went elsewhere, leaving their influence behind them. About the same time Jan Gossart was instructing young artists in the Italian style of painting historical scenes and nudes. With him "the Fleming became prejudiced by Italian influence."

More powerful in spreading Italian influences, but not always to the profit of native art, was Hendrick met de Bles. Other painters active in the first half of the century were Pieter Pourbus, Coeck van Aalst, and Hieronymous Cock. Coeck van Aalst's sketches of a trip he took to Constantinople illustrated subsequent editions of *The Arabian Nights*. Better-known artists who flourished in the next half of the century were Joris Hoefnagel, Henri Goltzius, Michiel Cocxie, Lucas and Marten van Valkenborgh, and Jan Cransse.

The Antwerp school, dominated perhaps by mannerism, was peerless in the use of pigments. Its members were superb colorists. Among the better ones were Hans Bol, a magnificent illustrator of animals, birds, and fishes; Gielis Coignet; Willem Key, who sickened when he saw Alva's face; Cornelis Molenaer ("Cross-eyed Neel"); Pieter Bonn, superb in watercolor; and Jacques de Backer, the best of the lot, a painter of carnations who produced highlights not only with white but with flesh color itself. Jacques de Gheyn was the Antwerp glass painter par excellence.

Antwerp also produced some able landscape painters. De Backer did landscapes in miniature, saying, "Let those who can imitate me now whistle on their fingers." Joos van Lierre had excellent landscapes in oils and watercolors, and Cornelis van Dale was a specialist in painting rocks. Molenaer, who worked with a maulstick, was unequaled in landscapes but had trouble with human figures, and Tobias Verhaeght and Jacques Grimmaer were much in vogue in this area. Hendrick van Cleef was highly Italianate. Adriaen de Weerdt, the deaf Hans Kaynot, Jan de Hollander, Martin de Vos, Joachim Patenier (who only painted when he needed money), Joos van Cleef, Gillis van Coninloy, and Joachim Buecklaer, who did kitchen scenes, were very good at landscapes and other types of painting and really deserve more than this brief mention.

The three most important Antwerp painters during the sixteenth century were Quentin Massys (1460–1530), Frans Floris, and Pieter Brueghel the elder. Only Floris was a native son, but the others had their most productive years in Antwerp, although one might argue—wrongly, I think—that such was not the case with Brueghel.

No one would dispute Antwerp's claim to Massys, who was head of the Antwerp school. "There is traceable in many of his [Massys's] pictures a foreign element perhaps coming from Germany and Holland, which came to be named after the painter Bles." He is best known, however, for his religious pictures. Unlike his rival, Hans Memling of Bruges, Massys was never satisfied to repeat what he had already done well. He moved from phase to phase, learning from every source accessible to him. Admittedly he had limitations, but his historical scenes foretold the mature Antwerp school of the seventeenth century headed by the incomparable Rubens.

Massys's life story has captured the imagination of romanticists. Orphaned at sixteen, he was forced to become breadwinner for mother, brother, and sister. He began as a blacksmith. A bronze medal bearing the head of Erasmus, the iron brackets supporting the font in Saint Peter's in Louvain, and the delightfully festooned iron well cover on the Handschoenmarkt in Antwerp are surviving examples of his craft. He probably left the forge because of an illness which made him too weak for the arduous task of ironmonger, although legend claims that his sweetheart, who later became his wife, complained about the dirt on his person and the noise of the forge. Whatever happened, he became the leading painter of his day and the intimate of Antwerp intellectuals and artists.

His paintings have a metallic quality, and although his composition leaves something to be desired, his details are superb even in an age famous for its skillful reproduction. His Virgins and women are endowed with all the charm that nature bestowed upon them, and his figures are very much human, rather than idealized. He put into historical and Biblical scenes the Antwerp and Antwerpians he saw in daily life. He was a true Netherlands humanist—a combination of the Italian and the Flemish. It is quite possible that he influenced the English portraits done by Hans Holbein. Frans Hals, Rubens, and Jordaens have in their works traces of his themes and techniques.

His name has been attached to a number of "burgher-pictures," which reflect the life of ordinary people—goldsmiths, lawyers, tax-gatherers, and Antwerpians at their business. Only two of this type are now extant: *The Gold-*

smith and His Wife (Louvre), and *The Thief and the Old Man* (Pourtalès Collection, Paris).

His skill brought him fame and prosperity, but unfortunately, many of his works have been lost. The two most famous extant paintings are *The Legend of Saint Anne*, done for the Fraternity of Saint Anne of Saint Peter's Church in Louvain and now at the Brussels Museum, and the triptych *The Entombment of Christ*, now in the City Gallery at Antwerp. The latter artistic gem has on one panel Saint John the Evangelist being boiled in oil and on another Salome presenting the head of John the Baptist to her mother. The central panel illustrating the Entombment shows Massys to be the most dramatic painter yet produced by the Flemish school. The figures taking part in the scene no longer appear half-indifferent to what is taking place nor do they appear half-demented. Massys received three hundred florins for this work done (1509–11) for the Cabinetmakers Guild for their chapel in the Church of Our Lady. It somehow escaped the "raving madness of the iconoclasts." Philip II tried to purchase it, and at one time the parsimonious Elizabeth I of England offered the staggering sum of forty thousand florins for it. In 1577 the Guild corporation decided to sell it, and the town magistrates bought it. It was "liberated" by the French revolutionists in 1794, but later was returned to Antwerp.

Frans Floris de Vriendt (*c.* 1517–70) in many ways is the most representative artist of the affluent, boisterous, and in some ways garish Antwerp of the sixteenth century. More than any other painter he reflected the "materialism and the feeling of successful well-being which animated" Antwerp "in the days of its prosperity." The term "florid" entered the English language when Frans was at his height and is probably derived from his name rather than from the Latin word *flora*, although his work is indeed flowery.

Today his work, with the exception of a few paintings and drawings, is not highly rated. Yet it was to his studio that the forerunners of Rubens came to mix the old Flemish manner of painting with the new Italian methods. His contemporaries considered him to be one of Europe's finest, and only the personality of Michelangelo overrode his own. He was praised in Antwerp by both Fleming and Italian.

Frans was a true Renaissance man. He loved to play; he loved to paint. Van Mander thought that his drinking habits adversely affected the quality of his canvasses. After a drinking bout, he would return to the studio, have the students pull off his boots, and start work. One night six topers came to Antwerp from Brussels to challenge him to a drinking contest. After all six had succumbed, Floris polished off a mug of "Rynschen Baey" standing on one leg. Another time he toasted each member of the Clothiers' Guild separately. He drank sixty times to their drinking twice. His students undressed him in the sumptuous bedroom with gold leather hangings of which he was so proud.

Later in life he had the stunning blow of seeing many of his paintings destroyed by vandals. A few survived because they were in Lucas de Heere's workshop. Of some of his famous altar pieces, we have only van Mander's description: "He treated all kinds of subjects in such a way that nobody has expressed better than he the emotions of the soul, sorrow, joy, and other effects. For this reason they call him the Flemish Raphael Urbino." Van Mander also felt that if Vasari had seen other than engraved reproductions of Floris's work, he "would have sounded his praise and eulogized him." Floris consorted with kings and princes, and along with his brother Cornelis, painter and architect, was a person of prestige in his native city.

Floris was also a brilliant teacher. Here he excelled all other Netherlands artists. His pupils "became surprising masters in all kingdoms and lands of Christianity," and may have totaled in number over 120. A figure is difficult to determine because the great Frans was freed from the customary obligation of registering his students with the Guild. His studio and school at one time had 30 painters. Among them were Martin de Vos, Lucas de Heere, Crispin van den Broeck, Martin and Henri van Cleve, Franz Pourbus, and the brothers Ambroise and Jerome Francken. To this could be added other names which together would make up a healthy roster of Netherlands painters. So excellent was his instruction that the works of de Heere have been confused with those of Holbein, and those of Franz Pourbus with those of Antonio Moro (1515–77).

Today Moro would replace Floris in a listing of the three greatest Antwerp painters of the sixteenth century. From an overall artistic viewpoint this is justifiable. Moro was an extraordinary portrait painter. Still he was not admitted to the Saint Lucas Guild until 1572, just five years before his death. To be sure, he was in and out of Antwerp and the Low Countries throughout his life, but Floris's complete identity with Antwerp and Flanders and his unique teaching abilities accord him his position among the "Big Three."

No one would contest the place of Pieter Brueghel the elder (1510–69). Admittedly he lived a part of his life in Brussels, but his training and much of his work, along with that of his sons and grandsons, link the Brueghel family to Antwerp and the Saint Lucas Guild there. Brueghel studied in Antwerp under Coeck van Aalst and Hieronymous Cock. He also spent a considerable amount of time during his formative years in Italy, where he acquired a naturalistic concept in his landscapes—a certain animism which pictured nature contaminating man, reducing him in stature and significance, continuing its ordered way regardless of his "joys and griefs, his dreams of glory and beneficence."

Of more importance, Brueghel, sometime during his studies, was exposed to the paintings of Hieronymous Bosch. Like Saul on the way to Damascus (which he later painted), Brueghel came so much under the spell of Bosch that in some ways he appears closer to the medieval masters than to those of the Renaissance as exemplified by Massys and Floris. For just this reason, Brueghel is important for the subsequent development of art in the Netherlands. He kept much that was good and predominately Flemish from being inundated by cheap Italian imitation.

Like Bosch, Brueghel treated things monstrous and deformed as symbols of moral corruption. Unlike Bosch, he never quite left the real world. Nature is always present in his work. Society is the real villain. In Brueghel, the maimed, insane, and poor rebuke the society that has dragged them down to the level of animals. Bosch in his greatest work had introduced spiritual terror by way of sexual excitement. Sexuality for itself is not explicit in Brueghel, and when sexual overtones are introduced, they more often depict man's foolishness and absurdities than his lusts.

More pertinent than whether Brueghel was medieval or modern is whether he was a man of his times. He definitely was that. Like many he was caught in the midst of the irrationality of his day. In religion he remained outwardly a conformist, but like Plantin was closely connected with Henry Niclaes and the Family of Love. His paintings to some may seem agnostic, but like the Family, Brueghel believed that salvation was possible only through love. To him love was all important, a life force, and it was impossible to isolate God from it. It is possible that he left Antwerp to go to Brussels for religious reasons, but his child bride was probably the reason for his going. Nevertheless, he instructed his wife to burn a number of his paintings after his death because they might bring religious persecution on members of his family, who were orthodox.

Brueghel's works reflect his era. *The Wedding Feast* has no more than twenty villagers in the room in compliance with an edict of Charles V which prohibited the gathering of more than twenty Flemings in a room at any one time. *The Massacre of the Innocents* is a *sub rosa* indictment of Alva and his troops and of Spanish atrocities. *Dulle Griet* ("Mad Maggie") points out the uselessness of war with the symbols of a political satirist.

His themes are universal. *The Procession to Calvary* is concerned less with the victim than with the baseness in the human character that allows people to watch with indifference while a fellow being suffers. *Christ and the Woman Taken in Adultery* is also a plea for charitable compassion. *The Numbering at Bethlehem* shows the indifference of the villagers to the miracle that is taking place, and *The Hunters in the Snow* shows men oblivious to all but the business at hand. The scenes were laid in the environs of Antwerp.

The dramatic touch in Brueghel's paintings appears in a somewhat different guise in the splendid canvasses of Rembrandt and Rubens. Brueghel, however, shows more sympathy for the lot of his fellow men. Like Rubens, Brueghel had "a tremendous gusto, a full-blooded heartiness and ebullient curiosity about the visual world, and an irrepressible appreciation of its physical satisfaction."

"Merchandise of no little importance"

How different he was from that other artistic colossus of the century, Michelangelo. Both were humanists; both were concerned with men. Michelangelo with his nude, muscular figures idealized man, but in so doing completely divorced him from reality. His Adam could never walk through the streets or inhabit a landscape.

Brueghel, the consummate Netherlander, did just the opposite. He glorified man not in his beauty, but in his plainness—by his link with the earth from whence he came, not by his association with angels. No matter that the body appears wrapped clumsily in rough ill-fitting garments. In any form but its own, it would lose its identity with nature. Brueghel, who fully comprehended the harshness of life, could not envision man out of the context of reality. *The Hunters in the Snow* and many of the peasant scenes illustrate this clearly. To Brueghel "when man breaks from nature, he becomes the victim of his own frailties. But Brueghel never accepted any human condition as proof that the cosmos is an accident—or that man's life within it is meaningless." Consequently, he treated "even human folly and vanity as unworthy of notice in the presence of eternal truths." To him there was a natural wisdom in the uneducated man.

This philosophy and the wisdom found in old Netherlands proverbs were basic to Brueghel's thinking. Like many of his contemporary countrymen—intellectuals like Erasmus included—Brueghel collected these proverbs, which, for the most part, were humanistic and sociological rather than theological. For example *The Magpie on the Gibbet* may have been based on "The way to the gallows leads through pleasant meadows." In Brueghel's paintings, the proverbs of his day are acted out by the masses in tavern, field, and village square.

John Canaday says that Brueghel's picturization of proverbs and parables makes the Netherlandish peasant a pantomimist. With a fine sense of balance, Brueghel never acts to extremes against the Italian mannerists. He refuses to sentimentalize "a lout as the symbol of virtue." Known as "Droll Pieter," he brought to his art sincerity, seriousness, and—above all—genuine humility. His drolls are curious and complex, but most of all delightful.

Brueghel took what was best from Italy, but primarily remained faithful to the old Flemish tradition, as did his sons and grandsons. The same was true of other Netherlands artists, who painted things as they saw them: flowers, pots, pans, fish, vegetables, musical instruments, people. Their canvasses reveal a careful observation and record of burghers, peasants, and nobles—their clothes and their possessions, their sins and their foibles, their laws and their customs. In so doing they give us a picture of sixteenth-century Antwerp. Furthermore, they lead the viewer to insights into the character of man, and in this they are timeless.

The people of Antwerp sought materialistic as well as spiritual values. Evidence of this could be found in the halls of the merchants, at the Exchange, in the building expansion of van Schoonbeke, and in the markets, tables, and kitchens bulging with food. Even so, the peasants of Brueghel, the victims of the bigots—both Catholic and Protestant—the syndices of the orphanages and hospitals, the people seizing power and those losing it, the scholars searching for truth and the printers publishing it had a common humanity that has transcended materialism and the passage of centuries.

Antwerp was good, bad, beautiful, and crass—truly Europe's greatest center of civilization up to the closing of the Scheldt River. Even then the city did not die. There were still Brueghels who painted and Plantin offspring who printed. Since then it has borne the armies of the French and the rockets of the Nazis, with enemy occupation in between. It has continued to survive, in spite of man as well as because of him. It has rebuilt where vandals have destroyed, and if need be, in an age of destruction for destruction's sake, it could build again.

Selected Readings

Branden, F. J. van den. *Geschiedenis Der Antwerpsche Schilderschool.* Antwerp, 1883.

Burbure, L. de. *La musique À Anvers Auz XIVe, XVe, XVIe Siècles.* Antwerp, 1843.

Canaday, John. "Bruegel," *Horizon,* Vol. IX, No. 1 (1967), 22–41.

Clair, Colin. *Christopher Plantin.* London, 1960.

Denucé, Jan. *Oud-Nederlandsche. Kaartmakers in betrekking met Plantin.* 2 vols. Antwerp 1912–13.

Durme, M. van. *Supplement Correspondence de C. Plantin.* Antwerp, 1555.

Geyl, Pieter. *The Revolt of the Netherlands.* 5th ed. London, 1966.

Guicciardini, Ludovico. *Description de la cité d'Anvers.* Anvers, 1920.

———. *The description of the Low Countries and of the Provinces thereof ....* London, 1953.

Mander, Carel van. *Het schilder-boeck waerin voor eerst de leerlustighe uieght den grendt der edel vry schildercenst in verscheyden deelen wert voorghedraghen.* Haerlem, 1604.

Prims, Floris. *Geschiedenis van Antwerpen.* Vol. XI. Antwerp, 1933–49.

Rooses, Max. *Christophe Plantin imprimeur anversois.* Anvers, 1882.

———, ed. *Correspondance de C. Plantin.* 8 vols. Antwerpen, 1883–1918.

———. *Musée Plantin-Moretus a Anvers.* Anvers [1894].

———. *Plantin et l'Imprimerie Plantin.* Gand, 1878.

Sabbe, Maurits. *Plantin, the Moretus and their Work.* Brussels, 1926.

Smedt, Oskar de. *De Engelse Natie te Antwerpen in de 16ᵉ eeuw, 1496–1582.* Vol. I. Antwerp, 1950.

Vinne, Theodore L. de. *The Plantin-Moretus Museum: A Printer's Paradise.* San Francisco, 1929.

Wauwermans, Henri Emmanuel. *Historie de l'école cartographique belge et anversoise du XVIᵉ siècle,* 2 vols. Bruxelles, 1895.

Wee, Herman van der. *The Growth of the Antwerp market and the European economy, fourteenth–sixteenth centuries.* Vol. II. (Univ. de Louvain. *Recueil de travaux d'hist. et de philol.*) Louvain, 1963.

Wegg, Jervis. *Antwerp 1477–1559, from the Battle of Nancy to the Treaty of Cateau Cambrésis.* London, 1916.

———. *The Decline of Antwerp Under Philip of Spain.* London, 1924.

Index

Index

Index